Side by Side

Side by Side

The Revolutionary Mother-Daughter Program for Conflict-Free Communication

DR. CHARLES SOPHY

with Brown Kogen

HarperOne
An Imprint of HarperCollinsPublishers

HarperOne

Some stories contained in this book are based on my patient experiences while others are composites of my work. They are provided herein to illustrate the points being made in the book. Names and identities have been changed in the interest of protecting patient confidentiality.

HarperCollins books may be purchased for educational, business, or sales promotional use. For information please write: Special Markets Department, HarperCollins Publishers, 10 East 53rd Street, New York, NY 10022.

HarperCollins Web site: http://www.harpercollins.com

HarperCollins®, 📖®, and HarperOne™ are trademarks of HarperCollins Publishers

FIRST EDITION

Library of Congress Cataloging-in-Publication Data
Sophy, Charles; Brown Kogen.
   Side by side : the revolutionary mother-daughter program for conflict-free communication / by Charles Sophy with Brown Kogen. — 1st ed.
   p. cm.
   ISBN 978-0-06-179157-4
   1. Mothers and daughters.   2. Communication in the family.   I. Kogen, Brown.   II. Title.
HQ755.85.S643   2010
646.7'8—dc22   2009023054

10 11 12 13 14   RRD (H)   10 9 8 7 6 5 4 3 2 1

Contents

PART THREE
Hot-Button Issues

Side by Side

Introduction

WITH ALL DUE RESPECT, I often compare the mother-daughter relationship to being on a roller coaster, the big, scary kind that you're able to see from the next town over and whose passengers can be heard shrieking from miles away. Parts of that ride can certainly be thrilling and crazy fun, much like the way you may feel when you and your daughter are really getting along. There may be other stretches of that same ride that leave you feeling anxious, fearful, or nauseated—much like the way you may feel when you and your daughter are in the midst of an argument. There's one big difference, though, between these two rides. Unlike the experience at the amusement park, the ride you are on with your daughter will never come to a halt, automatically release its safety bar, and allow you to exit. No matter how scary or intolerable the ride may get with your daughter, there's not even a chance of getting off. This ride is forever. And there is no safety bar.

The truth is, most moms don't really want to get off this ride. They'd just prefer a slower, smoother, more predictable journey, a ride with fewer upside-down loops or steep, heart-stopping drops— one that doesn't include, for example, your fifteen-year-old getting pregnant or your thirty-year-old becoming addicted to drugs. Nobody wants that ride. But it's a given that every mother-daughter pair faces challenges, and it's inevitable that at some point, there will be a challenge that will test the strength of this relationship and the ride will change.

Variables like genetics, personality, socioeconomic status, and family history will certainly inform the way moms approach these issues, how heated these potential conflicts become, and of course how they're resolved. However, aside from these variables, there is one significant factor that will give you and your daughter the best chance of negotiating these inevitable issues while maintaining an overall healthy and loving relationship: communication that is respectful and honest. This will not only ensure a safer ride, but will strengthen the bond between you and your daughter. This is our goal.

All mothers and daughters want the same things: love, under-standing, respect. And they want them from each other. Mom wants love, respect, and understanding from the child she brought into the world. And daughter wants the same from the woman who gave her life. Many moms seek professional guidance because their daughter is acting out in some way—such as getting a tattoo, dressing inappropriately, or dating someone the rest of the fam-ily deems undesirable. The specific behaviors may be age related, but they are simply the manifestation of the underlying desire to be understood, respected, and loved. The only real way that the mother-daughter relationship can evolve in a healthy, loving, and sustainable way is to satisfy these needs. And it boils down to com-munication, which is something that mothers and daughters are doing constantly, just not as effectively as they could.

The fact that mothers and daughters often struggle is certainly not a novel premise; a vast number of books and periodicals have been written on the topic, all in an effort to comprehend this potentially volatile dynamic. But none of them have offered the straightforward approach found in this book. The truth is, there is something you, the mother, can do to improve your relationship with your daughter. You have a chance, a really good one, to make it better. A lot better.

It is up to you. Why? Because you not only are the designated driver of your family, you are essentially the one responsible for the existence of your daughter in the first place. Whether conceiving a child was a conscious choice, a mistake that you ultimately chose to celebrate, or a journey through fertility medicine, you made it happen! You hungered to have a child and create a family, took the steps necessary to become pregnant or to adopt a child, and committed yourself to that mission. This in itself is a huge achievement. You may very well have a significant other who was part of that accomplishment—a husband, a boyfriend, a partner, an ex—and who remains part of your family unit as you journey through motherhood. If so, that person certainly has a role in the dynamic with your daughter. However, your relationship with your daughter must now be your exclusive focus. It is your responsibility to fully embrace the next challenge and figure out a better way to communicate with your daughter.

Most moms, due to fear or lack of resources, feel as if there is nothing they can do to improve their relationship with their daughters. Yet there is a technique you can use that draws on resources you already possess. With this technique, I have been able to make a difference in the lives of thousands of mothers and daughters. I call it the Chair Strategy. This simple and effective mom-driven tactic begins with a visual image of the position of two chairs. Imagine that these chairs represent the way you and your daughter are communicating. Are they situated back-to-back, with the two of you in a deadlock, unable to see each other's point of view? Are the chairs face-to-face, enabling each of you to share respectfully opposing viewpoints? Or are the chairs side-by-side, with the two of you working collaboratively to sustain your relationship? The answer to this question will enable you and your daughter to begin to understand how your communication efforts are succeeding or failing. The Chair Strategy will provide you with insight and tools to change the dynamic between the two of you, to more effectively resolve the conflicts that occur, and to emerge with an even stronger bond.

Whether your daughter is an infant or turns fifty years old tomorrow, whether the two of you talk several times a day or only sporadically, it is you, the mom, who must create an environment conducive to openness and true sharing. At this point, it doesn't matter whether the two of you fight with harsh words or clenched fists. All that matters is that you begin the process of working toward a healthier and more loving dynamic with your daughter. It is in your hands.

I hope you appreciate the power and importance you have in the relationship with your daughter. This fact informs my basic philosophy: Parenting begins with you. Not your child. *You.*

To explain this concept, I often use the analogy of the oxygen masks on an airplane. How many times have you heard a flight attendant utter the reminder that in case of emergency, you must first secure your oxygen mask and then your child's? In that context it makes perfect sense, right? When you're thirty thousand feet in the air and there's some kind of mechanical malfunction in the flight gear, you need to put your mask on first so you can keep breathing; only then can you help your child put on hers. So it is with moms and daughters here on the ground. Only after you are a balanced and secure woman can you model that kind of strength and security for your daughter. And as you embrace this philosophy, you will have an even more successful outcome with the Chair Strategy.

As medical director of the Los Angeles County Department of Children and Family Services, the nation's largest child welfare organization, I have treated this country's most vulnerable population. In my private practice as a child, adolescent, and adult psychiatrist, I have treated the nation's most privileged. I've seen, heard, diagnosed, and treated just about everything: infant malnutrition, depression, phobias, panic attacks from weight gain, addictions, and more.

My work is not limited to a traditional office setting either. I guide countless families on the spot by intervening on airplanes and playgrounds, on beaches and in parking lots—anywhere it seems appropriate. My family contends that I'm a crisis magnet, but I am drawn to this work because it is about making families stronger and, in my opinion, nothing is more important than family. My professional training—I'm triple board certified in Child & Adolescent Psychiatry, Adult Psychiatry, and Family Practice—enables me to care for my patients' physical and emotional well-being, including their most pressing emotionally based issues, the kinds of concerns that parents, children, and blended families face most often.

Twenty years and thousands of patients later, I can unequivocally say that of all the parent-child dynamics I've witnessed, none is more fascinating or frightening to me than that of mother and daughter. The breakneck speed with which the exchanges can travel from loving to toxic is even more intense than between most married couples in crisis. The collective power that fuels the intensity of the emotional extremes of mother and daughter is like no other. And the successful outcomes I have witnessed time and time again—regardless of the socioeconomic status or severity of the issue—are among the most rewarding and meaningful of my professional experiences.

Side by Side is meant to be a practical guide for every mom who wants to improve her relationship with her daughter by learning how to communicate in a more effective and loving way. Regardless of the age of your daughter, and whether or not you currently are on good terms with her, this book will equip you with the tools you need to make this happen. The book is divided into three parts:

Part One: The Up-Front Work focuses on you, the mom. It is a thought-provoking journey designed to help you gain strength, balance, and clarity in your life overall. You will be asked to complete numerous exercises and to consider various concepts as you create a personal tool kit based on your individual needs. Your honest efforts here will prepare you for the next part of the book.

Part Two: The Chair Strategy brings your daughter into the process and introduces the Chair Strategy. The exercises in this section will help you to implement the Chair Strategy while having some fun with your daughter.

Part Three: Hot-Button Issues puts all of the above ideas into practice as we look at the most challenging and contentious areas of parenting: sex, money, values, and divorce. It will introduce some mothers who have successfully dealt with these issues by using the Chair Strategy with their daughters.

In many ways, this book mimics the process I use with any mother and daughter who come to me seeking guidance. So as we begin our journey together, and I share my professional ideas and techniques, I ask of you the same as I would of them. Please embrace three concepts:

1. Commitment to learning about yourself and your daughter

2. Honesty when you are asked to participate

3. Trust in the process to bring you a positive result

If at any point you feel confused, frustrated, or downright angry at any insights, suggestions, or exercises in the book, know that you aren't the first person to question the process. Doubt and anger are common and sometimes necessary responses in order to move forward. But try to keep an open mind. The idea of no pain, no gain applies here. If you reach a point where you entertain the notion of stopping, don't! Instead, take a moment and remember:

Commitment. Honesty. Trust.

Not coincidentally, these are the three crucial ingredients needed to create and sustain a healthy and loving connection with your daughter.

Finally, before we begin, there are two specifics you should know about me. First, as a psychiatrist, my approach is (and always will be) strength-based. When I begin treatment with individuals or families, my first task is to help them identify their personal strengths, areas in their lives that are strong. By making the initial focus on the positive and the strong, the negative elements naturally and quickly begin to dissipate. In strength, there is hope. And within hope, I believe, there is tremendous power to guide you forward.

Second, I am a realist. I believe the particular circumstances of your life are what they are, and something you have to deal with every day. Many factors are beyond your control. That said, measuring the reality of your life against something you saw at the movies last week or on a rerun of *Gilmore Girls* is unproductive and pointless. These relationships, whether portrayed on the small or large screen, have been dramatized for entertainment purposes. The relationship with your daughter, no doubt entertaining at times, is real. And no matter what your reality is now, your goal of a stronger, healthier, and more loving connection with your daughter is within reach.

As a realist, I can't promise that you and your daughter will always be riding on that roller coaster together with entwined hands, joyfully shrieking in concert. But I can guarantee that your ride will be more pleasurable and that moments like these will become a distinct possibility.

Thank you for committing to take this journey.

—*Dr. Charles Sophy*

The Up-Front Work

You have huge power in the relationship with your daughter. Along with this power comes a responsibility to use it in the most positive and healthy way: honest and clear communication. This is the key to the best connection with her. And in order for you, mom, to meet this challenge most effectively, it is crucial that you first find your personal strength, balance, and clarity. This is what I refer to as "up-front work." By taking the time to do this work—before you focus on your daughter—the two of you will be that much closer to your goal of a healthier relationship.

Part One will guide you through this journey. As you get a glimpse into the lives of other mothers and daughters, you will be asked to look at your own life, reflect on the choices you make, and consider some adjustments. The up-front work you do here will help focus your magnificent power. And the more you offer of yourself in this process, the more you and your daughter will gain.

So roll up your sleeves, open your heart, and open your mind. Let's begin.

Strength

The Four Truths

Y OU ARE PART OF a very complicated relationship. You have a daughter.

The relationship may not be complicated at this very moment, but trust me, it'll get there. When I meet a mother who insists otherwise—and I have met a few—I'm skeptical. Given the fact that you are reading this book, you are probably not one of those moms. Still, if you wonder how it might be possible that your relationship with your adorable and devoted daughter could ever become contentious, I'd advise you to stick around. In my vast experience in working with mothers and daughters, each and every pair has gotten into trouble at one time or another. Yours will be no different; it can't be. The reason I am certain of this has absolutely nothing to do with you personally. Rather, it has to do with the fact that in every mother-daughter relationship, there are four inherent truths. They are out of your control. Despite what you are currently doing or not doing to facilitate better communication with your daughter, the Four Truths will ultimately make success more challenging.

1. Mothers and daughters want the same things: love, understanding, respect.

2. Mothers and daughters speak the same language.

3. Mothers and daughters, on some level, are in competition with each other.

4. Mothers and daughters have estrogen—lots of it.

Whether or not any of these truths hit home, I assure you that at some point each one of them will. Some moms don't believe in them until the havoc they have wreaked is apparent. Their dormancy may fool you into thinking your relationship is immune or that these truths don't apply to you. Trust me, each one of them is alive and well and will eventually rear its ugly head in an attempt to destroy your relationship. That is, if you allow them to do so.

I share these truths not to scare you, but rather to empower you. Awareness of them is the first step in giving you the strength to redirect their path from sabotage toward success in your relationship. On the face of it, the first two truths don't seem very threatening, and oftentimes they remain as simple givens to be aware of. Later on we'll discuss how even these apparently innocuous observations can lead to trouble. But first let's consider what each truth means.

Truth #1: Mothers and Daughters Want the Same Things: Love, Understanding, and Respect.

This truth is the cornerstone of your relationship with your daughter. If you believe nothing else, believe this truth! Every human on the planet, consciously or otherwise, desires love, understanding, and respect. Isn't that what you want? Of course you do, and so does your daughter. This truth is particularly easy to accept when the two of you are getting along well. But what about when you hit a rocky patch, when you are fighting miserably?

The challenge of this truth is to believe in its presence during times of conflict. The idea that you and your daughter want *opposite* things can be established very early in your relationship, and once your pattern of communication is set, it's very difficult to break. For example: It's lunchtime at the local mall, and I'm in line at the food court. A mother ahead of me orders a turkey sandwich and a bag of chips to share with her three-year-old daughter. Hearing the order, daughter begins to cry and whine that she wants a peanut butter and jelly sandwich. Mom tells her no. Daughter continues to protest by stomping her feet and screaming louder. Soon she's having a full-blown tantrum. Many patrons in the food court react in both discomfort and annoyance. Embarrassed, mom covers her daughter's mouth and snaps: "I told you, Jen, they don't have peanut butter and jelly sandwiches here!"

At that point, I notice a chalkboard menu above the order counter. Item #2 reads: *PB&J*. Mom turns to me, exasperated: "Do you believe this kid?" As I point to the menu and begin to speak, mom quiets me with a slight wave of her hand in my face and a knowing wink. Mom has now confirmed for me what I suspected, that she was aware they had peanut butter and jelly sandwiches but chose not to order one. Meanwhile, Jen continues to cry as mom pays for the food. The two head over to a table: an aggravated mom followed by her shrieking toddler.

On a superficial level, mom and daughter certainly want different things—one wants a turkey sandwich and the other wants peanut butter and jelly. But on a deep level, Jen and her mother—though at complete odds at this moment—want exactly the same things: love, respect, and understanding. Their poor communication creates a disconnect between them. Over time, these types of interactions will become habitual, hardening into a destructive pattern of communication. Let's take a closer look:

- Jen wants a peanut butter and jelly sandwich for lunch. She communicates this through a tantrum, which is perfectly age-appropriate behavior. If she did get her lunch request fulfilled, Jen would have felt understood and respected by her mom. In Jen's mind, having a need like this met equals love. This precedent was established and enforced from birth. Each time she cried in hunger or was in need of a diaper change, mom responded with a bottle or a clean diaper. There is no way that Jen could understand mom's unequivocal *no* unless it was accompanied by an explanation.

- Mom wants her daughter to have a turkey sandwich and communicates this by ordering her lunch, which is also appropriate. What is inappropriate is the way she has communicated to Jen about this. Mom lied, yet at the same time expects Jen to understand and respect her choice.

How is Jen to understand how to get or give understanding, love, and respect if mom is setting such a poor example? Do you see how this works against them?

The problem here is a lack of clear, honest communication. Both have every right to express their feelings. The truth is, though, only the three-year-old is clearly and honestly expressing the way she feels. Mom's response, while certainly clear, is far from honest. Imagine how these types of interactions can begin to wear down their connection over time.

A communication style based on deception will only serve to derail the relationship you have with your daughter. Communicating with honesty should always be the place you start with your daughter; otherwise, you're setting yourself up for real trouble. When mom is not forthcoming and honest about what is truly driving her, she is inadvertently sending mixed messages to her daughter. Clear, honest messages let your daughter know that not only is your behavior consistent, so too are the feelings you have—especially about her.

A patient of mine had a daughter who, from an early age, was enamored with chocolate. The daughter ate it constantly. The more mom tried to get her to stop eating chocolate, the more resourceful the daughter became in her search for it. Even though mom had long since stopped buying the candy, the daughter would find it at the homes of friends and relatives and would stockpile it so she had a secret chocolate stash in her room. At a loss about what to do, when her daughter was eight, Mom told her that chocolate could make you very ill, sick enough so that you could die. Unfortunately, the lie worked. So mom began to use this tactic to control all of her daughter's undesirable behaviors. By the time the daughter was thirteen, the list of activities that supposedly could kill you had expanded from eating chocolate to playing with big dogs and kissing boys.

When the daughter ended up switching schools, she made some new friends who quickly set her straight about the notions mom had been feeding her for all those years. This realization sparked frustration and disappointment over her mom's misguided protection and caused the girl to draw closer to this group of teens because, for the first time, she felt respected. Her tough bunch of friends was actually a gang that ended up leading the girl down a path of truancy and worse. While this real-life example may seem extreme, it does show that the older your daughter gets and the more significant the deception, the higher the stakes become.

With this in mind, let's return to the story of Jen and her mother. Here, the girl was left to cope with her anger and frustration. If this is the way they continue to communicate, two things will certainly happen:

1. Daughter will learn by example to shut out people and that trickery is acceptable.

2. Daughter's anger from being shut out will have to go somewhere. Depending on her age, it could lead her to rebel by acting out in various ways, i.e., experimenting with drugs, sex, etc.

This whole interaction bothered me, so I decided to insert myself into the situation.

After I paid for my lunch, I saw an open table close to Jen and her mom. Jen's tantrum had subsided, and at this point, she was sporting a sad pout. Mom was almost finished with her half of the turkey sandwich; Jen's was untouched.

Mom: You have three minutes to finish that sandwich, young lady.

I glanced at Jen as she picked it up and started to nibble. She caught my eye. I smiled at her.

Dr. Sophy: How's your lunch?

Mom: Fine, thanks. (Then to Jen) You have two minutes.

Mom had intercepted. Sadly, Jen continued to nibble. I tried again to connect to Jen.

Dr. Sophy: Not very hungry today?

Jen: I want peanut butter jelly.

Mom: That's all she ever wants. She's had it five times this week.

Dr. Sophy: Actually, I'm curious why it bothers you?

Mom: Why do you think? Wouldn't it bother you if this was your kid?

Dr. Sophy: Why does it bother you?

Mom: Because I want her to eat healthier. She never eats turkey; she needs to.

Dr. Sophy: So why not tell her that?

Mom: She's three.

Dr. Sophy: Yes, and clearly she understands a lot.

Just then, Jen interrupted and made my point.

Jen: Peanut butter six times!

I suggested to mom she empower her daughter with the truth and explained to her how next time she might convey this idea to her daughter in an honest and respectful way. She could say something like, "Jen, I know how much you love peanut butter and jelly sandwiches. I love them too. Since you've had so many this week, let's try something new. Turkey is healthy, and I love you and want you to be healthy." I explained to mom that even if Jen continued to protest, mom has done her job of communicating in a clear and loving way with her daughter.

Give Respect. Get Respect.
Give Honesty. Get Honesty.

It's natural for you, mom, to make decisions that don't meet with your daughter's approval. This is part of your job, and that's OK. What's not acceptable is to justify or explain these decisions with lying or deception. Though you may think you can get away with it, and you very well might in the short term, at some point your daughter will see right through the deception. Once your cover is blown, your credibility will be damaged. Even worse, she will be angry about it. This anger must go somewhere. Depending on her age, this anger may manifest in a tantrum or dangerous rebellion. And she will have learned from your example and will do the same to others.

Don't lie to your daughter. Be respectful. Be honest.

Once you internalize the truth that you and your daughter want the same things, you will perceive situations with her differently. Though it may require you to make some adjustments in how you approach her, over time these types of interactions will deepen the trust between you.

In summary, treat your daughter the way you would like to be treated. Be conscious of the fact that just like you, she wants love, understanding, and respect. By offering those things to her as much and as consistently as possible, you will get the same back from her.

Truth #2: Mothers and Daughters Speak the Same Language.

The common language—both verbal and nonverbal—that you and your daughter speak can certainly bring you closer when that language is respectful and loving. From the first days of your daughter's life, your caresses, hugs, and eye contact all communicated volumes to your newborn, and she responded in kind. Later on, when language comprehension kicked in, you began to develop a loving way of verbally communicating with each other, from using special terms of endearment to devising playful rhymes with her name.

This language also provides a safety net that is powerful and protective. Mothers everywhere communicate with incredible and precise shorthand—a glance, a gesture, a word, a head tilt—that indicates what is allowed, necessary, or to be avoided.

In addition, the idea that a mother always knows is something I believe in 100 percent. A mom's intuition allows her to look at her daughter and in a heartbeat know what's going on—that a cold is brewing, a boyfriend is straying, or an event didn't go as planned. The powerful connection created by this common language is a spectacular gift that moms and daughters enjoy.

In my generation, the adage "Sticks and stones may break my bones, but words will never hurt me" was a standard piece of advice that many parents offered to their children. It was certainly an idea my parents ingrained in me. For a long time, the catchy phrase empowered me when unkind words or remarks were directed my way. But it always seemed the idea was a big fat lie. Turns out, it was. Words can be devastating and damaging. Language, as we know, has the power both to hurt and to heal. And in the mother-daughter relationship, language can be lethal.

That same shorthand we mentioned above can also work against you. It is astounding to me how a seemingly insignificant comment or action can set off an argument between mother and daughter. An eye roll from daughter can do it. An "I told you so" from mom can too. These kinds of interactions happen all the time. It's easy to observe this kind of behavior when a mom and daughter are involved in the most basic activity, like shopping. Walking through a department store, for example, I saw a mom trying on lipstick samples as her twelve-year-old daughter watched. Mom tried on a shade of bright pink and asked her daughter for approval.

Mom: What do you think?

Daughter: Cool color.

Mom: Thanks.

Daughter: Maybe if you were, like, twenty years old.

Daughter giggles. Mom is visibly upset.

Mom: You are rude, young lady!

Daughter: Whatever. It looks dumb.

It seemed to me there was a long-standing dynamic here between this mom and daughter. Mom needs to acknowledge that she has either modeled this behavior or allowed it to be an acceptable way for her daughter to communicate. I'd also like to point out that the more you've incorporated Truth #1 into your parenting, the more freedom you have in Truth #2. If the mom at the makeup counter was more fully aware that both she and her daughter truly want the same things—love, understanding, and respect—and mom had modeled that behavior, this kind of sarcasm probably wouldn't enter into their interactions at all. And even if the daughter was sarcastic from time to time, mom would be better able to let it roll off her back rather than take it to heart.

Although the daughter said the lipstick looked dumb, what she was really telling her mom was something else. If mom was paying attention, she would know that either her daughter was tired and just wanted to go home or she was hungry or she was fed up because mom was always dragging her around to shop and at that moment she'd much rather be playing her flute, kicking a soccer ball with friends, or watching TV. Regardless, daughter provoked her mom with a rude comment rather than telling her exactly how she felt.

The subtle and not-so-subtle language between mother and daughter that delivers harsh criticism, sarcasm, and even verbal abuse is not developed overnight. It takes time, which is something the two of you have probably had lots of together. There is no doubt that each of you will become fluent in that language. If you're honest with yourself, you can probably remember the first time your daughter communicated something to you, verbally or nonverbally, that really got under your skin. Maybe it was a sassy hand-on-hip declaration: "You are a mean mom, and I hate you!" It may have even been an innocent remark that cut deep: "Mommy, that lady is fat like you!" Whatever it was, it made you stop and think for a minute, and it didn't feel so great.

Now let's try to get into your daughter's head. Have you ever provoked her? Maybe stood over her while she brushed her teeth and said "Side to side *and* up and down," or questioned her choice of skirt and top combination. It's quite possible—in fact, I'd put money on it—that you've said something that really got to her.

What's going on here is the slow creation of what are commonly referred to as buttons—the issues or sensitive areas that, when pressed, really get a person riled up. Over time, the two of

Button Pushing

When your daughter's language causes you pain, embarrassment, or hurt, your button has been pushed! Rather than react with extreme emotion, take a moment to realize this is a signal.

It's an indication to you that it's time to step up and teach your daughter a better way to express her own feelings so that, in the future, she doesn't hurt others' feelings. The moment you react with negative or extreme emotion, you will alienate your daughter and push her further away. Of course, you may be hurt; you are human. But what's most important here is that you show your daughter a better way to communicate. You have just been handed an opportunity to do this.

you develop quite an array of them. And you both become master provokers with the goal of getting attention. The more a mom pushes her daughter's buttons, the more the daughter will eventually push mom's. Over time, each of you learns which buttons really do the job. Every mom and daughter pair has a unique assortment. In the example above, when the daughter told her mom that the lipstick color she chose looked dumb, what she may really have been doing was pushing mom's button, the one marked "Feeling insecure about my looks."

The best way to approach this truth about language is with an awareness of what you're saying. The more you speak with sarcasm or disrespect toward your daughter, the more it will come back to you. And the more you speak with respect and love, the more that will come back to you, too. Regarding the makeup counter incident, it would have been better if mom responded to her daughter's comment by telling her exactly how she felt, and maybe even expressed her vulnerability by asking support from her daughter. For example:

Mom: That wasn't the answer I was expecting.

Daughter: Well, I don't like it. You asked my opinion.

Mom: Yes, I did ask your opinion because I value it. And you certainly don't have to like the color. Maybe, though, there is a better way for you to let me know it's not a good color for me.

Daughter: OK, like how?

Mom has now honestly expressed that her feelings have been hurt (a button has been pushed), and she has responded with truthfulness. In doing so, she has accomplished several goals:

- Setting up a healthy and honest framework for her and her daughter

- Redirecting the path of communication

- Teaching her daughter that honest communication is important, but it must be delivered respectfully

Truth #3: Mothers and Daughters, on Some Level, Are in Competition with Each Other.

This truth is a tough one to see, much less accept. It sounds terrible and, to some moms, it's downright insulting. How could it be that you and your daughter are competing in some way? This is the girl you love unconditionally, and the person for whom you would do just about anything. Sure, you can imagine a friendly competition, maybe even a major battle over Monopoly, but that's not what I'm talking about here. I'm referring to the subtle and not-so-subtle competition that's not necessarily acknowledged overtly but simmers right below the surface, just enough to cause trouble.

At this point, I hope you can agree that you and your daughter want the same things—love, understanding, and respect—and that you two definitely have a special way of communicating. Based on that connection alone, the stage is set for the potential of competition because at some point the two of you would naturally want *other* similar things, such as attention from the same person. Can you see how it is the perfect setup?

The initial appearance of this truth can occur when your daughter is quite young. The idea of daddy's little girl—when mother feels in competition with her daughter for her husband's affection—is the classic example. For the secure and confident mom, a daughter becoming the apple of daddy's eye can be a relief. Finally, you get a welcome break and a bit of space. And having dad as a loving, strong force in your daughter's life is ideal . . . unless you believe that he has shifted his primary attachment from you to your very own daughter.

As your daughter gets older, your issues with each other can get more complicated. And it goes back in part to how you were mothered. We'll talk more about this important relationship later, but for now, let's look at how this history can trigger competition between you and your daughter. If your own mom was a packrat, for example, and your childhood home resembled a small warehouse of periodicals and magazines, you may very well be taking great pains to keep your house pristine. Newspapers, magazines, and the like are recycled daily. Dishes belong in the dishwasher. No dirty laundry is in sight. You get the picture. As a result, your daughter has grown up with a long list of rules and regulations that she finds oppressive. When she leaves for college, guess what kind of housekeeper she is going to be. A packrat, just like your mom . . . It's not that your daughter necessarily takes pleasure in taunting you with her stacks of paper; rather, on some level she is saying to you, "I've got a better way!" It's the same message you were giving your mom, consciously or not.

Other forms of competition exist. Moms are always encouraging their offspring to try new experiences, including some of the passions that have fueled their lives—anything from traveling to bargain hunting or cooking. But as a daughter starts to establish her independence and identity, she may unknowingly tread on her mom's turf, which can definitely turn into an unwitting competition.

Suppose mom has spent her entire life perfecting her double chocolate cheesecake recipe. It's the family favorite, her claim to fame. Daughter has watched mom make this since she was a toddler, cracking dozens of eggs and licking hundreds of spoons for the cause. She's learned all she knows about baking from mom, and as an eighteen-year-old has created her own signature dessert, Oreo Pie—the *new* family favorite. Something as simple as this could make mom feel as if her status has slipped; she has been demoted from dessert chef to kitchen detail, particularly if one of mom's unmet needs has to do with her cooking accomplishments or achievements as a housewife. For daughter, based on the fact that mom taught her everything she knows, she probably expected nothing but a beaming smile from mom regarding her pie triumph. Do you see how this leads to unconscious competition?

It is only natural for a mom to want her daughter to succeed, whether it's academically or socially. It's part of her responsibility to be supportive of her child's goals. The trouble begins when a daughter, again in an effort to strike out on her own, may disregard the path mom has encouraged. At that point, mom may decide to accept her daughter's alternative choice. Or mom may choose to reject it with envy and anger. This is when the gloves come off and the woman versus woman battle can emerge in full force.

For example, a mother and her seventeen-year-old daughter are lifting weights at the gym. The topic turns to the daughter's new boyfriend, Josh. Not only does mom approve of him, she points out that Josh reminds her of someone she dated in college. Mom tells her daughter: "Josh looks almost identical to this guy Michael. Same hair, same build, same butt." They share a giggle. They may be giggling now, but what happens when mom seems to be flirting with Josh? Or is actually flirting with him? Or in an extreme version, actually seduces Josh? Not so funny.

The best way to face this truth is with your own clarity about who you are. The more you know about yourself and what you stand for, the better equipped you will be when competition creeps in. This is part of the up-front work we'll be doing later in this section of the book.

Truth #4: Mothers and Daughters Have Estrogen—Lots of It.

You've heard the jokes about "that time of the month" when a woman starts crying at an AT&T commercial, wants to strangle her husband, bite off her own fingernails, or tell a waiter to shove it because her french fries and chocolate shake are taking too long to be served. The true culprit in these instances is a hormone, specifically, the hormone called estrogen—one of the biggest causes of mood swings, anxiety, and physical pain for all females. And you and your daughter have it. In abundance.

Often called the sex hormone, estrogen is produced primarily in the ovaries and is instrumental in the development of sexual and reproductive organs, as well as the regulation of the menstrual cycle. But its impact on the body is much greater: it also affects the urinary tract, bones, breasts, skin, heart, blood vessels, and hair. Estrogen protects against heart disease by reducing cholesterol levels, is believed to decrease the incidence of stroke, and may even help protect against arteriosclerosis and even Alzheimer's disease. Sounds pretty good, this estrogen, and it is, for the most part.

Yet the reason why estrogen belongs on the list of Four Truths is because its most significant effects are on a woman's body and brain. Fluctuating levels of estrogen can trigger physical pain, such as menstrual and ovulation cramps, and headaches. It can cause mood shifts too, particularly increased anxiety, rage, and sadness. Conditions like these can easily affect the way a woman feels and therefore interacts with others. Both you and your daughter are going through these changes at different times and to varying degrees . . . no wonder it can be tough for the two of you to get along. Estrogen is like that acquaintance of yours who loves to stir things up, whose sole purpose in life seems to be to show up, un-announced, and cause trouble.

Thanks to the advances in reproductive technology, women are able to bear children well into their forties, and sometimes beyond. And there is always adoption. With women starting families later in life, the paths of estrogen in a mother and daughter intersect at different and often more "lethal" points. It can be challeng-ing to be a mother at the low end of her estrogen production—menopause—parenting a teenage or young adult daughter at the height of hers. Or toilet training a toddler while having severe hot flashes.

Just be aware and respectful of the fact that, as women, both you and your daughter have bodies full of estrogen and this can

Tool #1: Strength

1. Mothers and daughters want the same things.

2. Mothers and daughters speak the same language.

3. Mothers and daughters, on some level, are in competi-tion with each other.

4. Mothers and daughters have estrogen.

Be aware of these truths. Allow them to empower you.

affect the way you communicate. If you can, try to step back and understand that your common "friend" is sometimes to blame. This awareness may help ease the situation for the two of you.

You should now have a better understanding of the inherent challenges you and your daughter face based on the Four Truths that naturally exist in your relationship. Many of the confusing and frustrating interactions with your daughter may start to make more sense now that you are aware of these truths. I hope so.

As you move through this first section of this book, you will explore various concepts in order to gain strength, balance, and clarity in your life. Through journaling, questionnaires, and other exercises, you will work with each concept to tailor it to your specific needs as a woman and as a mom. Ultimately, each one of these personalized tools will help you to improve your relationship with your daughter. Recognizing, understanding, and personalizing these tools are exactly what the up-front work is about.

The Four Truths comprise your first tool. Reflect on these truths and keep them in your tool kit forever.

What follows is an exercise to bring you back to the moment when you first laid eyes on your daughter. Getting in touch with this moment will mark the beginning of our up-front work together, which will continue in the next couple of chapters. If possible, start with a fresh pad of paper or notebook and keep it throughout our process together. At the end of this book, you will have a personal journal to look back on.

For now, I'd like you to focus on when these Four Truths came into your life, the moment you became a mother. This was your first true connection. Regardless of whether you gave birth to your daughter, adopted her, or had a surrogate bring her into this world, the moment you saw your daughter for the first time was, no doubt, a powerful and life-defining one. And you accepted this responsibility forever. Whether your daughter is currently an infant, a toddler, a teenager, or an adult, remembering that initial connection with her is where I'd like you to begin this journey.

EXERCISE: FIRST LOOK

The goal of this exercise is to reconnect with the most powerful moment of your life: the first time you laid eyes on your daughter and could physically touch her skin.

The exercise begins with a ten-minute relaxation or meditation period followed by guided journaling about the experience. You might want to read through these instructions before you begin.

Preparation

1. **Quiet time:** Commit to ten minutes of uninterrupted quiet time. It could be any part of the day—morning, afternoon, night—whatever you choose. Try to pick a time when you have the greatest chance of being uninterrupted. This is *your* quiet time.

2. **The place:** Choose a soothing place, indoors or outdoors, where you can sit or recline. Although it may not be realistic that you'll be perched on a mountaintop or near a mesmerizing waterfall (if you can, lucky you!), the place you choose should offer a sense of peace and tranquility. Maybe it's a place that holds fond memories for you and your daughter. Choose whatever will help you relax most.

3. **Get cozy:** A chair, a couch, the floor, the grass. Soften your surroundings with pillows, blankets, or anything else that makes you more comfortable. Loose or unrestricted clothing will help you get even cozier.

4. **Music:** If you choose to play music during this exercise, keep the volume low so it is not distracting.

Meditation

Once you are set up and completely comfortable, take in your surroundings. After a moment, set your phone or a timer so it will sound in ten minutes. Close your eyes and continue with the following:

1. **Slow and deep breaths:** As you sit quietly, begin to take slow and deep breaths.

2. **Focus on your breathing:** You can do this by envisioning air going through your entire body. Inhale and exhale; breathe deeply. Try to make the exhalation even longer than the inhalation. Continue to focus on the exhalation. Feel the air leaving your body.

Try not to hurry through this time. As you relax, reflect on your journey that ended with the first time you saw your daughter. Consider some of the following days and specifics of the path. Allow yourself to remember these events as they were, the joy and the pain:

1. **The day you chose to begin the journey:** Whether you conceived naturally, with artificial insemination, through IVF, adoption, or surrogacy, think about the time of your life when you chose to begin the journey toward the manifestation of your daughter. What was going on in your life at the time? Think of the actual reasons why you wanted a child. What were your expectations at that point? With whom did you conceive your daughter? Think about that person, how you met, your first touch.

2. **Getting pregnant:** Think about this process as a whole. Remember its simplicity or its complications. If you conceived naturally (and know the actual day), think about that experience. If your process was complicated, what was the reason? How did these complications make you feel—frustrated, fearful, resigned, sad? What were some of your biggest emotional

and physical upsets along the way? Did you ever have a miscarriage? A string of months when you couldn't conceive? A failed attempt at artificial insemination? Other disappointments? Were you alone through this process? What helped you to get through these events and keep on going?

3. **The day you found out you were expecting:** If you were pregnant, how did you find out? How did you feel when you first heard the news—elated, scared, upset? Did you have physical symptoms, and if so, what were they? Who was the first person you told the news to and what words did you use? What was that person's reaction to the news?

4. **Remember the process:** If you were pregnant, think about the highs and lows you experienced, such as the first ultrasound, other tests, morning sickness. If you went through the adoption process, domestically or internationally, think about what was required of you to complete the process. How were you feeling during this time, both emotionally and physically?

5. **Last-minute anticipation:** Think about the last few days— the homestretch—before meeting your daughter. Were you happy, scared, anxious, full of regret? Were you nervous that you wouldn't be a good mother? If you were pregnant, were you scared about the actual labor and delivery?

6. **Birth day:** If you gave birth: Were you prepared? Was it a rush to get to the hospital on time? Or was it a slow process with a few false alarms? What were your contractions like? What was the delivery like and did it go as planned, or was there a change in plans—a cesarean, for example, or an emergency of some kind?

7. **First look:** Remember everything you can about the first time you saw your daughter. Every detail of her face, her nose, her eyes, her cheeks, her mouth. Her hair. The smell of her. The

sound of her cry. The way she felt. The way you felt when you kissed her, the way she looked then.

Meditate on these powerful and life-affirming details.

Guided Journaling

Write down the feelings and thoughts you had while meditating. You can write simple words and adjectives for each entry, or more elaborate descriptions. This is yours to refer to as you make your way through this book, and it is something you will have forever as a keepsake.

Balance

The Key to Your Life

I N THE PREVIOUS EXERCISE, were you able to go back in time and experience your daughter's birth again? Could you remember the special details of that glorious event? Though my hope is that these recollections conjure up the initial elation you felt for your blessing, these memories may also serve as a harsh reminder of how life has changed since then, how far apart you and your daughter have grown, and how exasperating she can be.

That's OK. Before we go any further, I'd like you to air your grievances about your daughter. No, this is not a trap. It may surprise you that a psychiatrist would ask you to do this. Let's be real, though. Chances are, you didn't reach for this book because you and your daughter have a blissful relationship. I'm not saying there aren't aspects of your relationship that are good. But truthfully, if you were sitting in my office right now, you'd be telling me what's really on your mind, and it's more than likely that you'd start by complaining about your daughter. No worries; it's why we're here. You are safe.

The top ten complaints I hear from moms are:

1. My daughter won't listen to me.

2. I really don't like her sometimes.

3. My daughter needs medication.

4. She needs to see you daily, Dr. Sophy.

5. My daughter's clothes never look good.

6. She chooses rotten friends.

7. She refuses to eat with us.

8. She hates the entire family.

9. She only listens to her friends.

10. I'm afraid of my daughter.

Depending on the age of your daughter, the complaints about her might vary. If she is an infant, it could be that her wailing or erratic sleep patterns are becoming unbearable. If she is a toddler, it could be her willfulness or her serious tantrums. If she is a preteen, it could be her attitude or her testy language. If she is an adolescent, it may be that she's been hanging out with a rough crowd or showing signs of drug use. If she is an adult, you may feel she is too permissive (or too strict) with her own kids. Or, like the mom I met at my child's school, you may think your daughter is just plain crazy.

As I waited in the carpool line, I heard the honking of a car horn. I looked over at the car next to me; the driver motioned for me to roll down my window. Though I didn't know her, I assumed the driver was a mom whose child attended the school. I rolled down my window.

Mom: Hey, Dr. Sophy, I think my kid is going crazy. Seriously, she needs help.

Her tone was serious; she laughed nervously.

Upon hearing the *crazy* reference and noticing a four- or five-year-old child in the backseat, I offered a pointed comment:

Dr. Sophy: I don't think you mean "crazy" . . .

Mom: Yeah, yeah, she's just not making sense.

It was important to make the point about mom's inappropriate word choice. I told her to call my office and we'd talk.

On the average, I receive about five calls a week from parents who voice some kind of complaint about their child. Typically, it's a mom calling—scared, frustrated, or raging—about something her daughter did or is threatening to do—getting a tattoo, piercing her tongue, or becoming a vegetarian. Once I've determined we're not dealing with a true medical emergency, my response is always the same: "Before I can figure out what's going on with your child, I really need to meet with you first. I want to spend some time with you, the parent." The reason for this request is simple, and it is my basic philosophy: Parenting begins with you. Not your child. *You.*

Self-Fulfilling Prophecy

There is never an appropriate time to refer to your child as crazy. Period. Comments like this cut deep, particularly when they come from you. They undermine a child's self-esteem and call into question the trust she has placed in you. A parent's evaluation means a lot to a child and falls hard on her. If you believe that telling a child "Great job" has a positive effect on how she views herself (which it does), then you must know the opposite is also true. Tell a child she's crazy or fat or selfish and guess what . . .

The philosophy that parenting begins with you is not about blaming or pointing a finger at you (or anyone else) for your child's difficulty. Rather, this strength-based philosophy encourages the parent to respect, love, and take care of herself first and foremost. Yes, that means you come first in the relationship with your daughter. Does this make you uncomfortable? Does it sound selfish? There's actually nothing selfish about it. In my opinion, not putting yourself first is selfish. Why? Because putting yourself first means that you value your own life and recognize the importance of taking care of yourself. This is the only way you can stay healthy—emotionally and physically—so that you can be a good role model for your daughter. There's nothing selfish about that!

Carpool mom did call me the next day. Like most moms who call, she was resistant to the idea of coming in on her own and insisted it was a huge waste of time. I understand completely why a mom would feel this way. Here she is, desperate for help with her daughter, and I'm asking her to take the time to have a private chat with me first. It's as if mom sliced her hand open, and I'm suggesting we stop for coffee on the way to the emergency room.

I know these moms are metaphorically bleeding when they call. Right now, you may be as well. But it's essential that the initial meeting be with mom; it's the first step in understanding the family dynamics.

On the phone, the lady from the carpool explained to me that her daughter was stressed out about starting first grade and it was affecting her daughter's sleeping and eating patterns, which in turn made her cranky most of the time. Several days later, mom came in to see me. As I anticipated, she was a nervous wreck. She was the one overwhelmed that her "baby" was about to start full days of school. Yet she couldn't make the connection between her own feelings and her daughter's behavior.

In her words, "I never let her see me upset or uptight. I'm really good that way."

Then she unraveled in my office. There is no way that a mom so clearly upset could possibly be hiding this kind of emotion from a child. Still, she simply refused to see how her own anxiety could be affecting her daughter.

I suggested that both mom and daughter come in for the second session. They walked in like two peas in a pod: same True Religion jeans, diamond stud earrings, and hairstyles. As the daughter spoke to me, quite articulately in fact, mom continued to interrupt, translating what she believed her daughter was really saying. I gently explained to mom several times that there was no need for her to intervene, as I didn't require the extra help in order to understand her daughter.

The session ended and the daughter went to the bathroom. As soon as she was gone, mom asked: "Don't you think a little Xanax would do the trick?" I explained to mom that medicating someone, particularly a young child, is something I would only do as a last resort. What I wanted to say, but couldn't, was: "If anyone's anxiety could benefit from Xanax, it would be yours." But I did remind her, "Parenting begins with you." Then daughter returned, and they left.

It was in the next session that mom finally understood my message. Even if mom thought she was hiding her concern, her daughter was internalizing the emotions that were clearly radiating from her. Once mom was able to deal with her own anxieties and feel more settled about this new phase in her parenting life, her daughter's behaviors and mood improved. A stronger, more resilient mom almost always equals a stronger, more resilient daughter.

Here's something else to consider: Being a strong parent means not only taking care of yourself so you can be an effective parent, but it also means staying firm in your parenting convictions so your daughter isn't receiving mixed messages. Don't say no or yes to her request for an expensive pair of jeans, a second helping of ice cream, or a plea to stay out until one a.m. unless you mean it without any reservation. The trouble arises when your response isn't completely accurate—when your *no* or *yes* is really a *maybe*. Your uncertainty or anxiety affects her. If your daughter asks if a friend can sleep over and your response is maybe, this is frustrating to her. What does *maybe* mean, exactly? It's not clear, it's not the answer she is looking for, and it can make her anxious. On the other hand, if you say yes, follow through and allow it. Don't just say it to appease her. Be honest. Stay strong.

Parenting Begins with You. Not Your Child. You.

If you haven't already done so, embrace this philosophy of putting yourself first. Give yourself permission to take care of yourself so that you are operating from a position of balance.

Finding Balance

If parenting begins with you, then you owe it to your daughter to be the best you can be. I believe the foundation of the best possible you is balance. Life doesn't discriminate when it throws out curve balls. At some point, we will all experience setbacks of one kind or another. If your equilibrium is not on its game when this happens, you will be far less equipped to handle these challenges.

So how do you begin achieving balance in your life to be the best possible you? Do you have any idea what the best possible you even looks like? Let's begin by taking a close and honest look at the five key areas of your life. These areas will tell you everything you need to know about your emotional, intellectual, spiritual, and physical well-being. I refer to these key areas as S.W.E.E.P.™, an acronym that stands for:

Sleep

Work

Eating

Emotional Expression of Self

Play

S.W.E.E.P. is a simple, easy-to-remember checklist and can help you evaluate how you're doing. When a patient comes into my office for her initial visit, the first activity I do is ask about what's going on in each of these areas. I do a S.W.E.E.P. on them. A balanced S.W.E.E.P. makes the difference between an emotionally and physically stable mom and a walking disaster. It doesn't matter who you are, what you do, where you live, or how much you earn, if three or more of these areas are out of whack, you are not functioning at the top of your game. Even if one area is seriously askew (for example, you've been suffering from insomnia) this too can make a big difference. And if your life is out of balance, your daughter is going to suffer.

Do you have a vision of what a mom with a balanced S.W.E.E.P. looks like? It's probably not what you would think. Some of the patients with the worst S.W.E.E.P. come into my office looking like they have it all. On the outside they appear to be balanced, and many even think they are, but once they sit down and we start to talk about their lives, it is shocking what is often revealed.

When thirty-three-year-old Christi came to see me for the first time, she was dressed in a beautiful cream-colored linen suit with her hair and makeup done, as if she were headed to a photo shoot instead of a psychiatrist. With a confident, no-nonsense air, she strode into my office and sat down. As always, I began by asking her what was going on in the five key areas of her life. Here's what I learned.

Sleep: She had insomnia so she needed to take several catnaps during the day to keep herself going, including when she was waiting to pick up her daughter from school.

Work: She was a stay-at-home mom and miserable that she had no income and no place to go each day.

Eating: She had battled bulimia for most of her life.

Emotional Expression of Self: She'd been married for seven years and hadn't had sex with her husband for the last four of those years.

Play: She had one friend she did most everything with socially; however, this friend was a drug addict.

So much for the appearance of the picture-perfect life, right? The components of S.W.E.E.P. are life supporting. It continues to amaze me how out of touch many people are with these five key areas of their lives and how oblivious they are to their importance. S.W.E.E.P.ing yourself is a big piece of your up-front work.

Let's take a closer look at the five key areas of S.W.E.E.P.

Sleep

Your body needs it, in both quantity and quality. You should be spending about a third of your life sleeping, but I bet you don't even come close! So many of us are overwhelmed, overscheduled, and overloaded that sleep seems like the easiest commitment to give up. But how do you expect to think clearly and to handle all of the challenges of work, life, and parenting without sleep? It's not possible. And you will suffer because the more exhausted you are, the greater the chance you'll become irritated, make poor decisions, or even get physically ill. That lack of sleep trickles down to your daughter too, since it means you can't be there for her anywhere close to 100 percent. Be honest, how often does your daughter get a grouchy (exhausted) mom who doesn't have the patience to listen to her problems or help with her homework?

The more your sleep habits are out of whack, the greater the likelihood that your daughter isn't sleeping so well either. Then you have a cranky mom trying to get a cranky kid to school. Or worse, an inattentive mom letting her daughter make bad life choices.

Consider this: If sleep is not a priority for you, chances are you are not paying close enough attention to your daughter's sleep. Certainly, then, she's not learning the importance of sleep from you. Sleep is a big deal.

Work

If you work outside of the home, it is often the case that your colleagues become like a second family to you since you spend more time in the office than almost anywhere else. The forty-plus hours devoted to work every week should bring you satisfaction at least 75 to 85 percent of the time.

For many of us, of course, work is an economic necessity. But consider this: If your employment doesn't truly fulfill you in some major way—professionally, financially, socially, personally—you couldn't possibly be happy when you come home at the end of the workday. This lack of fulfillment may lead you to take your frustration out on your family.

You may be working with specific financial goals in mind, such as buying a new car or taking an exotic vacation. Could these be more important to your family than having a contented and healthy mom? If that is why you are working, what kind of message does that send to your daughter about money and its importance? On the flip side, you may have chosen to be a stay-at-home mom because you felt it was the right decision, but it wasn't necessarily what you really wanted. Your attitude about your work affects everyone in your life.

Eating

If you think the only problem with eating poorly is weight gain, think again. You can always go down a dress size, but you can never replace your family. The danger of bad eating habits is greater than simply nutrition or cholesterol levels. Eating can be a wonderful social activity as well as an excellent time for the family to bond. You should be sitting down with your family for at least three meals a week. Every time you gobble down food in your car while racing from one activity to another, you are sacrificing not only your health, but also the chance to share a moment with your family.

Consider this: Eating time is bonding time. It is the perfect opportunity to sit with your daughter, look her in the eye, converse, and share stories about her day and yours. How we eat, what we eat, when we eat, and where we eat can make the difference between a physically and emotionally connected mother and daughter, and a relationship in disarray. Get it while you can!

Emotional Expression of Self

Examining emotional expression offers a true window into mom's psychological state. Expression of self is the essence of soul. In my experience, when mom's emotional life is compromised in some way, her relationship with her daughter is often strained too. If mom is angry with dad or upset about the direction her career is heading and does not express it (or deal with it appropriately), these repressed feelings or the emotions that have been only superficially addressed have the potential to affect her daughter. Expressing emotions and allowing others to express them is the key to a healthy mother-daughter dynamic.

It sounds simple, but this is not always true. Think about it, do you really express yourself? Do you show public displays of affection toward people you love? And if so, how do you typically do it—with silliness, sarcasm, rage, or joy? Expression of self also includes whether or not your own emotional and sexual needs are being met. And once again, your behavior sends a distinct message to your daughter. Do you have an intimate relationship with your husband, boyfriend, or life partner? Are you emotionally connected? Are you dissatisfied, angry, or sad? Do you express these feelings, or do you try to suppress them? True anger and sadness, when not expressed outwardly, often becomes self-directed, which is the definition of depression.

Consider this: It has been said that without the freedom to express ourselves, we would shrivel up and die. So imagine a daughter who doesn't feel comfortable enough to react with true emotion, or a mom who has trouble verbalizing what she's feeling.

Connecting Your Head to Your Heart

On a train ride from New York City to the suburbs, a mom sits next to her six-year-old daughter.

Mom: We'll grab lunch after we visit Nana.

Daughter: Nana's not coming to lunch?

Mom: No, she's very sick.

The daughter nods but says nothing. She looks down, then turns to her mom.

Daughter: I feel really sad about Nana being sick. Do you?

Mom looks at her with a vacant face, then hands her a book.

Mom: Here, why don't you read until we get there?

This exchange hit me hard. Upon hearing her grandmother was seriously ill, the child immediately felt and expressed sadness over it. In her head, she *knew* grandma was sick. In her heart, she *felt* sad. She connected these two things—her head and her heart—in an instant. This may seem basic to you, but it's not. Her mom certainly couldn't do this. Mom's response to her daughter's question was evasive, revealing nothing about what she was thinking or feeling regarding her own mother's impending death.

The ability to connect your head to your heart is one of the most significant steps in self-expression. It helps you to communicate in the most effective and healthiest way with others, including your daughter. Having this ability means you are present, in the moment, and aware of what's going on around you. It is a great skill and a gift you'll want to pass on to your daughter.

Connect your head to your heart.

Play

If expression of self is the essence of our soul, play is the nurturing of that very soul. It is the vehicle by which expression of self comes out. Play is your release, although it is not to be confused with sex or intimacy. Rather, play provides feelings of fulfillment and joy in other ways. It can be a hobby, exercise, dating, or any outlet that provides fun, excitement, and hard-earned sweat. You, mom, like all of us, are a child inside, and that child needs to get out and be nourished. If that playful part of you gets suppressed, you are more likely to get angry, depressed, and frustrated. Play is your reward for all the hard work you do, and that includes paid work as well as the many other responsibilities you shoulder.

Think of play as the nutrition your psyche needs to enable you to grow and develop as a person. It supports your ability to be resilient and make good decisions, and it adds flavor to your life.

Putting S.W.E.E.P. to Work

Now that you have a better understanding of what each area of S.W.E.E.P. encompasses, it's time to do a self-assessment or, as I like to say, it's time to S.W.E.E.P. yourself. Below is an exercise that will help you to consider these five areas of your life. (Later on, I'll ask you to consider your daughter's S.W.E.E.P.) This exercise will not take much of your time, but it does require your honest and sincere thought. You will not be graded or judged, and probably no one will even see what you've written. But I have faith in your commitment because, as a parent myself, I know there is no better motivation than working to improve your relationship with your child.

Regardless of how often you assess yourself by using S.W.E.E.P., the real importance lies in being aware of these different areas. Balance won't happen overnight, but awareness alone is a big step. And as you begin to build on the strengths in your S.W.E.E.P. and pay more attention to areas that need to be bolstered—a topic we'll cover a little bit later—you'll achieve a greater equilibrium and this stronger, sturdier sense of self will have a marked effect on your daughter. It will show her how you prioritize these basic areas of your life. And once your S.W.E.E.P. gets stronger, the quality of time spent with your daughter and your connection to her will improve.

Tool #2: S.W.E.E.P. Checklist

Sleep

Work

Eating

Emotional Expression of Self

Play

EXERCISE: S.W.E.E.P. YOURSELF

The goal of S.W.E.E.P. is to achieve balance in your life. By looking closely at these five key areas—sleep, work, eating, emotional expression of self, and play—you will see the importance each plays in contributing to that balance. And collectively, you will see how a strong S.W.E.E.P. will make a huge difference toward becoming the best possible you.

In your journal, record your responses to the following questions:

Sleep

How much sleep do you get on an average night?

What one word best describes the way you feel in the morning when you wake up?

Do you sleepwalk? Sleeptalk?

Do you hit your mate or objects during your sleep?

Do you cry out or scream?

Do you dream when asleep?

Do you remember your dreams?

Do your dreams feel like they're part of your day?

Are they happy? Scary?

Is there a common theme to your dreams (such as being lost in a crowd)?

Do you look forward to bedtime?

Do you have a routine before bed? If so, what is it? Does the routine involve another member of your family?

Do you need to read before falling asleep? Watch TV?

Do you get ready for bed at the same time each night?

Are you the first or the last one in your house to get ready for bed?

Are you the first or the last one up each morning?

Do you nap?

What clothing do you sleep in? Do you have a reason for that choice?

Is your bed comfortable? If you sleep with someone else, is the bed the right size for the two of you? Is it a place you look forward to being in at the end of a day?

When you walk into your bedroom, do you feel a sense of comfort?

Do you love your sheets and pillows?

As you sleep, do you hear disturbing noises or distractions—traffic, television, snoring?

Is the temperature comfortable in the room where you sleep?

Is the room you sleep in used for anything else, such as work or watching television?

Work

What are your job duties? Are they what you thought you were hired to do?

Is your work fulfilling? Do you see tangible results from your work? How do you feel about those results?

What are your goals at work? Are you achieving those goals?

Do you view your current work as a stepping-stone to something else or as the place you really want to be? If it is a stepping-stone, what are you working toward?

Do you have friends at work? If so, do you have a chance to socialize or eat lunch together?

Are you confined in a cubicle all day?

Do you have windows in your office?

Is there tension at work between you and others?

How is your relationship with your boss? With your subordinates?

Do you socialize with your co-workers outside the office?

Do your family issues seep into your time at work? Does this bring stress?

Does your work financially reward you? If so, are you satisfied with that compensation?

How did you get your job (e.g., educational training, word of mouth, via a relative or friend)?

Do you feel appreciated and respected at work? If not, why?

Do you work at more than one job outside of the home?

If you are a stay-at-home mom, how many hours a week are spent on that work?

Eating

Do you eat regularly throughout the day? At what times?

What do you eat?

Do you enjoy eating?

Do you have a favorite food or type of food? How often do you get to eat it?

What prompts you to eat (hunger, headache, time of day)?

Do you skip meals? Are you constantly dieting? Do you go without eating for an extended period of time?

Do you get irritable when you don't eat?

Do you overeat? Do you binge then purge? Do you eat or eat more when you are emotional (anxious, sad, happy, etc.)?

Do you think food is vital to maintain good health? Do you think it's a mechanism for survival?

With whom do you eat?

Which types of eating experiences do you enjoy: with family, alone, with friends, at home, in a restaurant, at someone else's home?

What role do you play in your family's eating (planning, shopping, cooking, cleaning up, coordinating schedules)?

Do you eat with your family at least three times a week?

Do you and your family talk with one another when you eat? If so, is it chitchat or deeper conversation? What are some of the topics you talk about?

Do you feel a real connection to your family during mealtime?

What room do you generally eat in?

Is the TV on during mealtime?

Are there any other activities going on around you during mealtime?

Emotional Expression of Self

Are you involved in intimate relationships, both sexual and emotional?

What is fulfilling in those relationships?

What is not fulfilling in those relationships?

Do you have sexual desire?

How do you handle feelings of rage, sadness, fear, happiness, disappointment, and frustration?

Do you know intellectually when you are feeling any of these emotions?

Are your heart and head connected during that process?

How do you express these feelings to others?

Do you cry, laugh, and smile?

Are you able to control these emotions or do they get out of hand?

Play

Describe what is fun for you to do.

How often do you have fun?

Have the activities you consider to be fun changed over the years?

Is your daughter the only person you have fun with?

Did you pick these activities or hobbies or did they pick you (e.g., school volunteer duties)?

Do you share these hobbies/activities with your friends? Or do you do them alone? Do you have a preference?

Do you exercise? If so, how regularly and what type of exercise?

Is there any exercise you would like to be doing but can't seem to find the time for?

Do you see your friends in a social setting?

Do you spend any alone time caring for yourself (such as getting a massage, preparing a special meal, reading a book for pleasure)?

EXERCISE: S.W.E.E.P. FOLLOW-UP

Now that you've considered the previous questions and jotted down your responses, you should have a general idea of which areas in your life are strong and which ones could use some shoring up. This is not a one-time exercise but an ongoing process. We human beings are always growing and adapting as our circumstances change. In order to make the necessary adjustments in your life, you might find it helpful if you begin by taking an even closer look at the areas in your life that are strong (remember that my approach is strength-based). Say, for example, you begin each day feeling well rested. Maybe it's because no matter what is going on in your life, you always make sure you're in bed at a reasonable hour—whatever that means for you. And you have always taken the time to make your bed every morning—fluffing up the pillows, keeping a scented candle by the bed—so that, whenever you happen to walk into the bedroom, you are always greeted with a pleasing sight (and smell). No wonder you always look forward to sinking into your bed at night!

How might you use this same approach to change another area of your life where you're feeling less balanced? For example, between working full time, managing the children, and running the house, maybe you can't imagine how you could possibly whip up a healthy dinner and eat it together as a family. You sometimes joke that your car is an adjunct dining room. Since you do find the time to keep your bedroom looking so nice, perhaps you could designate a few times a week when everyone could eat together at home, even if the food isn't prepared in your kitchen. And maybe every Sunday morning the family could make brunch together, with an emphasis on healthy and nutritious fare? Try it and see how it goes. It may inspire you to sit down for more meals together, or at least with most members of your family.

Now that I've given you some ideas on how you might approach making some adjustments, here are some additional suggestions to keep you moving in the right direction:

Sleep

Try to get at least seven to eight hours a night.

It helps if your pre-bed ritual is pleasurable or, at a minimum, not another series of chores you have to do before going to bed. If your nighttime routine includes activities like paying bills, change the routine!

Do you feel as if you're keeping yourself up because you're hesitant to go to bed? If so, you may want to check with a doctor to see if there are any medical reasons preventing you from sleeping, such as anxiety.

Be sure the space feels inviting—consider the room temperature, the sheets you sleep on, the scent in the air, and the level of noise around you. If your partner snores, encourage him or her to find out why and address it.

Work

Try to make work as stimulating and engaging as possible.

Having good relationships with your colleagues makes work more satisfying, so be sure to take a break every now and then and socialize.

If you are dissatisfied professionally and want to make a career change, begin by talking with your partner, a friend, a trusted colleague, or a career counselor and making a plan for your future. But be patient! It takes time to make this kind of shift.

Eating

As often as possible, try to eat together as a family.

Whether you're dining with your family, friends, or solo, *enjoy* what you are putting into your body. Make healthy food choices and remember that poor ones can weigh you down, physically and emotionally.

It's not just about the food. Make mealtime an occasion to reconnect, share stories about your day, reminisce about past experiences, and tell jokes.

Emotional Expression of Self

Be sure your head and heart are connected.

Express yourself to others; let them know you love them.

Be sure to blow off steam appropriately.

Don't forget to cry.

Don't forget to laugh.

Build in time for emotional and physical intimacy.

Play

Try to find time to enjoy yourself on a regular basis.

There's nothing like learning a new skill to keep life interesting. Take a class, read a book, learn to knit or do needlepoint, try to master a new sport or activity. All the better if you can do this in the company of others.

Along similar lines, stay involved and active: join a book club, neighborhood choir, community theater group, or folk dance club.

It really is OK to pamper yourself every so often.

If your daughter is your only real playmate, broaden your circle. It is never a good idea to place your child in the role of fulfilling this basic need; it is your responsibility to yourself.

Whenever I first talk to people about focusing on their S.W.E.E.P. and making some changes in their lives, I inevitably hear some variation of the following:

- "Sounds good, but I don't have time for this!"

- "My daughter will only be young once; I want to spend as much time with her as I can. I can always _____ (insert your weakest area here: sleep, eat better, and so on) later."

- "I would love to find some time to go out with my husband, but my daughter gets so upset when she's with a sitter, I couldn't possibly leave her for an evening."

Don't be swayed by these excuses. Keep your eye on the dual prize: a more grounded, balanced *you* and an improved relationship with your daughter. It's up to you, although—as will be discussed in the next chapter—it is actually your unique and imperfect self that your daughter really needs to see. As you start to recognize and embrace your idiosyncrasies, you'll be amazed at what an even better role model you will be for her. And in time this can lead to an even stronger relationship with her.

CHAPTER

Clarity

Your Daughter, Your Opportunity

ONE OF THE MOST FREQUENT WORDS that a mom uses to describe her newborn daughter is *blessing*. Whether that daughter was conceived during a careless night on the beach, after years of fertility treatments, through an adoption, or from a good old-fashioned act of love, most refer to her—at least initially—as "a favor bestowed by God, thereby bringing happiness." A blessing.

At some point your feelings start to change, as you well know. You may be trying to figure out why your "blessing" is driving you nuts or if she was actually put on this earth as a test. Of course, this is not true. Yet, at the same time, the difficulty you are having with her is most likely what led you to this process with me. I believe that it is during these periods of frustration or anger that you come to realize that your daughter (aside from being a blessing) is an opportunity. A true and valuable one.

By definition, *opportunity* means "a situation or condition favorable for attainment of a goal." So then, what goal could your

daughter possibly help you to attain? The clarity of who you are
as an individual, as a mother, and as a woman. In many ways, this
happens naturally as you parent your daughter. Her actions—and
reactions to you—will in turn cause you to view yourself from
a different perspective. The feelings you experience as you wit-
ness your daughter's triumphs and struggles can help you to gain a
greater understanding about yourself. If watching your daughter's
jubilant face opening gifts on Christmas morning makes you feel
miserable rather than happy, this is something to take a closer
look at. Ditto if you are a divorced mom and your daughter's en-
gagement to the man of her dreams causes pangs of jealousy or
makes you uncomfortable or fearful for her.

Embrace this idea: Your daughter is a magnificent opportunity
to figure out who you are and what you stand for. It is all part of
the process of gaining clarity about yourself so that you can fully
share that aware, authentic, and satisfied version of *you* with your
daughter.

Your daughter sees you in a way that no one else ever will. She
came into this world captivated by your every move, every sound,
and every touch and believing there was no one more beautiful or
capable than you. You are the star of her show, an event that began
when you first held her. At that point, you became her primary
caretaker and the spotlight turned on you, where it will remain for
a long time. Certainly dad or other family members share it but,
quite frankly, you are perceived as the star performer in her life.

Even before she was able to speak, your daughter assigned meaning to each word you spoke and every action you took. She will
never stop doing this. All choices you make send a message that
will affect her in significant ways. The idea that your daughter's
eyes are on you can be scary. Don't let it be. She doesn't need
perfection. Nothing even close. What she needs is the authentic
you, the real you who makes choices that speak to your passions.
And yes, that authentic self includes all the quirks and idiosyncrasies and weaknesses that make you who you are. Your obnox-
ious laugh, poor spending habits, dry sense of humor, tendency to

About That Opportunity . . .

Let me underscore a few points here. For starters, wanting this opportunity should never be the reason for having a child. It just happens to be an often-overlooked perk. Second, a woman who never has a child can of course become a whole, completely centered, and best possible version of herself. Third, even the most solid and stable woman can get thrown off balance with the arrival of a child. It is part of human nature—and actually quite ironic—that often the catalyst that initiates the imbalance (the daughter) is also the opportunity that ultimately helps her recapture that balance.

interrupt—even your inability to sew on a button—are all part of your charm.

The role model you provide for your daughter is one that only *you* can supply, as it is based solely on your unique self. So take some of the energy you've been spending on fulfilling your daughter's needs and shift the focus to yourself. In taking care of yourself and your needs, you will see that her most important need is being fulfilled. And that need is for you to be your authentic self. She deserves this. So do you.

Think back for a moment to your childhood. I'd be willing to bet there are scenes involving your own mother that are etched in your memory, but if you asked her about those events, she wouldn't even remember them.

A twenty-year-old patient of mine, Erin, was having a rough time with her mother regarding her boyfriend. Erin had brought him over to the house for mom to meet, and she felt mom was rude and inattentive to him. Mother and daughter, now barely speaking, sat in my office to figure the situation out.

Erin: You were rude to him, Mom. That's how you are.

Then she turned to me.

Erin: She pulled the same stuff with me as a kid.

Mom: What are you talking about? What do you mean by "the same stuff"?

Erin's parents got divorced when she was little, and she lived full time with her mom. In our session, Erin spoke about what it was like to grow up in this environment. She felt her mom was often preoccupied, particularly during mealtime, and it had always bothered her.

Mom: Inattentive? I was there every night at dinner!

Daughter: No, you cooked and fixed me a plate. You never sat with me at dinner, ever. Ever.

In mom's mind, she had been present every night. Erin's recollection was of her mom being there physically but unavailable emotionally because she was either on the phone or watching TV during dinner. This gave Erin the feeling that even her own mom found her too boring to sit with.

Just like Erin did with her mom, and you once did with yours, your daughter is observing and learning from your every move. If you think you can somehow manage to cover her eyes during the less flattering parts of your show, you are mistaken. Even when you attempt just that—to cover her eyes, metaphorically speaking—she takes that into consideration as well, sensing that if it's something you are keeping from her, it must be pretty darn important. She's a smart one, that daughter of yours. So you need to be clear, extremely clear, about who you are. This is the opportune time to be clear. You have the ultimate motivation. Your audience awaits.

One afternoon I received a text marked *Urgent* from Jane. At the time, I had been treating her for two months for a shopping addiction. Her treatment was going well, but she did have occasional panic attacks. The last attack had been two weeks prior and was triggered when she drove by her favorite store in Santa Monica and saw a sign in the window that read *50% Markdown on All Jewelry.* I assumed this text was a similar cry for help; I called her back immediately. She answered the phone extremely distraught.

Jane: This is so bad, Dr. Sophy . . . It's horrible.

Dr. Sophy: Please, Jane, tell me what's happening.

Jane: It's Matty. She said something awful to me.

Matty was her five-year-old daughter. Jane and I had talked about her a lot, though Matty and I had never met. I knew she was in kindergarten and, according to Jane, was keeping pace with her peers academically and possessed a sharp wit.

Dr. Sophy: Tell me what Matty said.

Jane was sobbing at this point, barely understandable. After a moment, she collected herself and told me what had happened. The two of them had been in Jane's bathroom, chatting and looking in the mirror together as Jane brushed her hair.

Matty: You are so pretty, Mom.

Jane: Thanks, honey, so are you. Look at you . . .

Matty: Nah, you're prettier than me on the outside, Mom, but I don't care 'cause I am so much prettier than you on the inside.

No wonder Jane was so upset! As hard as it was for Jane to hear Matty's comment, ideally Jane should have received Matty's words in a calm way. (Unfortunately, this wasn't the case. Instead, Jane reacted by telling Matty how mean and rude she was, then broke into tears and sent her to her room for the night.) If she had not allowed her own emotions to take over, Jane would have opened up a path for further dialogue; the message to Matty would have been: "You can tell me anything. Your thoughts are safe with me." Then Jane could have gently prodded Matty. For example, she might have said, "Tell me why you feel this way." While it's not always easy to respond with equanimity, doing so now will lay the groundwork for future (and even more difficult) conversations that are bound to come up.

The next week when Jane came in, she admitted that this comment from Matty cut so deeply because it rang true. And for her, it was a wake-up call. Jane knew she was extremely concerned about her physical appearance; she also acknowledged that she was often short-tempered and downright rude to those around her. This is why Matty felt mom was not so pretty on the inside. Jane knew that it was time to figure out why her physical beauty seemed so much more important to her than what was on the inside—especially because she had always told Matty that the opposite was true. Matty's comment had given mom an important piece of information—and an opportunity to examine her own actions.

Now it is your turn, mom. Your daughter has given you the same opportunity to figure out who you are and what you stand for. One of the ways you can do this is by taking an honest look at what needs of yours have not been fulfilled. These needs must be addressed so they do not stick around and interfere with your relationship with your daughter.

Mom's Needs

To illustrate my point, let's use a simple example. Suppose on some level you've never gotten over the fact that you didn't make the cheerleading squad in high school. Whatever it was that you hoped to gain by making the squad—acceptance, status, or an opportunity to show off your skills and have some fun—it didn't happen. That need never got fulfilled. So guess what? It's still there, somewhere. You may think you've long since put that high school trauma behind you, but if you never truly addressed this loss, the desire that was never sated will pop up again. On the surface it may look differently, but that hunger for acceptance or attention has not gone away. And not coincidentally, it will emerge at a time when it really should be in check—like when your daughter is contemplating a run for student council or the cheerleading squad or when she's involved in a sport, as in the following example.

Kelly, the mom of an eight-year-old girl named Lola, had been a gymnast as a child. Though she won several medals for her talent, Kelly never got the recognition she felt she deserved. When Lola was two, Kelly signed her up for a gymnastics class. Lola enjoyed tumbling but didn't share her mother's passion for the sport. Nonetheless, Kelly continued to push her. By the time Lola was six years old, she had definitely achieved some success with gymnastics on the local level, but mom wanted her to compete on the national level.

When Kelly came to see me, their relationship was in trouble. Lola had started to talk back to her mother and had even slapped her on occasion. Kelly was furious at this disrespectful behavior but couldn't see the connection. She didn't feel that Lola's aggression was a reaction to the fact that she kept pushing her daughter to excel in the sport. Though Kelly agreed that gymnastics was important to her, she refused to accept the idea that her unmet needs in this area were causing her to push Lola.

The first time I met Lola, I could see how physically exhausted she was, with dark circles under her big blue eyes. She told me she missed her friends. The turning point for Kelly was several weeks later. The morning of a major competition, Lola had woken up very congested and with a high fever. Kelly insisted that Lola get dressed and attend the event. Lola was miserable. As Kelly backed out of the driveway on their way to the gym, she caught a glimpse of Lola in the rearview mirror. She was shivering and crying but trying to be brave. That was the moment when Lola stopped paying for Kelly's disappointment with her own gymnastics career. Mom reversed the direction of the car and took her daughter back home.

As Lola's story illustrates, Kelly allowed her unresolved feelings to get in the way of her parenting. When this happens, your insight and guidance—important parts of your job as mom—will be affected. You will not be working in the best interests of your child. As a parent, your focus should be on your daughter and what makes sense for her. (This is all subconscious, by the way. None of this is malicious.) Let's consider another example.

It was the day after Mother's Day. I had just wrapped up a keynote address with about a hundred moms. A few of them had stayed to ask me questions. One was an anxious woman who wanted to talk about her nineteen-year-old daughter, Michelle. She was a college sophomore, a straight-A student who was majoring in art history. Though she had never been out of the United States, Michelle's dream was to one day own an art gallery overseas and fill it with magnificent pieces from artists she had studied and admired. Just the day before, though, Michelle had announced her decision to take a year off from college and travel through Europe. She planned to return the following year and finish her studies. Mom referred to her daughter's announcement as "throwing a bomb at me on Mother's Day." At this point, they weren't speaking. I wanted to understand why mom was so devastated by this news.

Dr. Sophy: Why does her decision bother you?

Mom: Are you kidding? What if your daughter did that to you?

I asked her about her own college experiences. She explained that she had never been to college. Her parents couldn't afford it; it was never an option.

Tool #3: Clarity

- Know your personal needs and unresolved issues.
- Be aware of how these needs and issues drive your behavior.
- Try hard to keep your needs and issues out of interactions with your daughter.

Mom: Why do you think I've spent my entire life working and saving every penny? Not so little Missy could screw it up, that's for sure!

Her feelings were intense, not so much toward Michelle as about her lack of options when she was her daughter's age. Mom's loss over never having the opportunity to attend college was still eating away at her. Not until she understood and addressed this could she begin to analyze rationally her daughter's announcement.

EXERCISE: UNMET NEEDS

Now it is time to take stock of your past. Think about the major regrets and disappointments you have, events in your past that you can no longer change. Below is a list of questions to consider. As you reflect on each of them, try not to put any kind of *judgment* on the feelings these questions evoke. Instead, notice your reactions. What are they telling you? Take your time; this is hard work! Record your thoughts in your journal. When you are finished, you will have a written account of your unmet needs. This will also serve as a reminder to you: These needs have no place in your interactions with your daughter.

Consider the following:

1. **Your mom:** How would you characterize your relationship with your own mother? Do you wish it had been different? Do you wish she had been a different kind of mother? Do you wish you'd been a more attentive, understanding, or tolerant daughter? How was her relationship with your father? What lessons did you glean from their interactions?

2. **Childhood:** Do you look back fondly on your childhood? Are there specific memories that have stayed with you—about your grandparents or extended family, grade school, a family vacation, or your favorite pet? Are there choices that, if you'd

done differently, might have made a big difference in where you are today?

3. **Teenage years:** Were you an experimenter, a conformist, or something in between? Would you change anything about how you spent these years? Were you a diligent student, or did you goof off a lot? Did you have ambitions that were never realized?

4. **College:** Do you consider this time the best years of your life, as the saying goes? Were you intellectually engaged in your studies, or did you feel as if you were just passing time in class? Did you declare a major out of passion or necessity? Did you have an active social life? A steady love interest? Did you experiment a lot with sex, drugs, or alcohol? Do you feel as if you went to an institution that was a good fit for you, or do you wish you had chosen a larger/smaller/different kind of university or college? Are you still in touch with your college friends?

5. **Early adulthood:** Did you pursue the career choice and other activities that you had thought you would? What is the dream versus your reality?

6. **Career:** Think about the jobs you've had and the path of your career. Were these jobs just a means of support, or were they intellectually engaging? Have you held a series of jobs, or have you worked at the same company for a substantial period of time? Did you push yourself to move on to the next stage of your career, or did you stay in a job because of inertia? Do you now regret having quit a job on impulse? Are there employment opportunities you wish you'd had?

7. **Love life:** Think about your significant romantic relationships. As you consider each one, write down the following:

What do you wish you had done differently?

How would you have preferred that relationship to end?

Unresolved Issues

It bears repeating: The problem with unmet needs, aside from the difficulties they cause for you personally, are the confused feelings they can elicit that might cloud your judgment in your role as the parent. Your personal feelings—based on your own loss or existing needs—must be set aside; they do not belong in these conversations with your daughter. Ultimately, this causes most of the worst conflicts between the two of you. Why? Because anything less than clarity about yourself will translate into trouble. The minute your daughter senses this confusion on your part, it becomes an opportunity for her, consciously or subconsciously, to push your buttons and challenge you. This is not a confrontation you want to have. Chances are, you will lose, and lose big.

What did you learn from this relationship?

What was great about it?

8. **Travel and other experiences:** What is the one experience of travel that you've always wanted but have never had? Are there other life experiences you feel you have missed out on?

9. **Marriage:** Before you got married, what did you imagine your life would be like? How is that life different from your current reality? Do you wish you had married a different kind of person, or that you had been a different kind of partner? Maybe more accepting? Less judgmental? Something else?

10. **Motherhood:** Before you had your daughter, what did you imagine your life would be like? How is that life different from your present life? Do you wish you could have been a different kind of mother? Less restrictive? Less anxious? More impulsive? Something else?

11. **Recognition:** Are there area(s) of your life in which you have not gotten the recognition you feel you deserve?

12. **Body image:** As a child, were you considered too skinny or overweight? Is that still the case (objectively speaking)? How do you feel about your body? Are there parts of it you would like to change? Have you spent a lot of time thinking about your body, exercising to lose weight or stay buff, or consulting with doctors, nutritionists, and the like to perfect your physical shape to the way you want it?

Nobody's Perfect

Everyone has a past, and everyone has her pimples; it's part of what makes us who we are. So stop feeling bad about this. One of the biggest challenges a mom faces is being a strong and appropriate role model while at the same time being true to herself—even if that includes engaging in what some would view as questionable behavior. There are a lot of gray areas in life—if only it weren't the case—and it's up to you to decide which habits and actions you will accept and which you'll shun in your position as a role model for your daughter.

For example, how does a mom with a young child send the message to her daughter that drinking can become an addiction if mom enjoys an apple martini at dinner with her husband, going out with her friends for a few rounds, or curling up at home with a good book and a glass of chardonnay?

How does a mom wear a body-hugging dress, one that she's worked extremely hard to fit into, and at the same time convey to her daughter the importance of modesty and self-respect?

How does a mom eat a dinner of two corn dogs and a hot fudge sundae with her kids and still stress the importance of good nutrition and a healthy diet?

The journey of self-discovery you are currently on will help you find the answers that are right for you. No one will judge you or your decisions as long as you choose them from a place of strength, balance, and clarity. These choices will come into greater focus as you complete your up-front work.

You Are the Tree

There's an old saying: "The apple doesn't fall far from the tree." I'm sure you've heard it. Symbolically, of course, the apple represents the child, and the tree, the parent. The phrase basically asserts the continuity of family characteristics, both good and bad, and that our children, despite everything we do or don't do, typically become like us, the parents. Yet most people never consider this message from a slightly different perspective. Let's take another look:

The apple doesn't fall far from the tree.

I say, "Thank goodness it doesn't!" You, mom, are the tree. You are the biggest influence on your daughter. And who, may I ask, better than you? Who better to show her the way? Who better to help her navigate the many tricky roads she'll encounter, especially during her first eighteen years of life? Nobody.

If this idea makes you feel uneasy, perhaps it's because you believe that being the tree implies you must be perfect or, at least, better or more capable or something closer to the stereotypical mom. Wrong.

Being the tree, in my opinion, means being the strongest and most authentic version of you. Even if you are a mom who doesn't love being a mom or who has real vices, you can still be the perfect tree for your daughter, not by changing, but by actually owning and acknowledging who you are.

Embrace yourself, mom. You're a great tree.

Your Mom

It's dinner hour at a neighborhood restaurant. A group of eight forty-something women are having a girls' night out. The enthusiastic conversation and laughter—even when just placing their orders—is infectious. Simply put, these ladies are having a great time, and everyone else in the restaurant can sense it.

At some point, one of the women walks away from the table to take a call on her cell phone. Moments later she returns, visibly annoyed. She tells her friends the call was from her mother (who was babysitting), asking her to stop on the way home and pick up some bananas. "So irritating," she says, referring to her mom and the request. There is supportive recognition from the others in the form of smiles, chuckles, and eye rolls.

"So are you going to stop on the way home?" one of them asks.

"No way," she facetiously snaps. "I told her, 'Get your own bananas, lady!'"

The group lets out a collective roar. It is clear that they all understand the intense feeling behind the sarcasm toward "mom." It is equally clear that they all know that their friend has every intention of stopping for those bananas. Conversation continues among them, and one of the ladies suggests that, just for fun, they go around the table and each say one word that sums up their mom.

"That's it. One word," she explains.

The game commences, and the following words are spoken as each takes her turn:

"Selfish."

"Nagging."

"Mean."

"Crazy."

"Controlling!"

"Deaf."

"Bitchy."

"Manipulative."

Does this shock you? For me, it confirms the universality of the mother-daughter relationship. Similar to the stereotypical way women often talk about men ("They're all jerks!") and husbands ("They're all lazy!"), there seems to be an accepted idea in our culture that moms—aside from the unconditional love they provide—are extremely irritating and overbearing. And can be quite amusing to poke fun at.

Back at the table, the game ends and the women start chatting again in groups of two or three. One woman remains silent. Then she quiets the group and slowly begins to speak.

"Hey, you know what?" she says. "There's one word no one mentioned that could actually describe all of our moms."

"What is it?" someone asks.

The woman takes a teary breath, smiles gently, then quietly says: "Alive."

There is complete silence.

"All our moms are still alive," she smiles. "Do you realize how lucky we are to still have our moms in this world?"

It was a powerful moment. Most of the ladies got misty-eyed, squeezed each other's hands, or made contact in some way. One simple yet profound word touched each one of these women. The love and deep connection, healthy or otherwise, they had with their moms hit them hard.

This moment was also a testament to the power a mom has over her daughter. You are that mom! And just as your own mother informed your actions and values, you are shaping the way your daughter will mother her own child. To help you think more specifically about any of the unresolved needs that are a product of how you were mothered, take a few minutes to complete the following writing exercise.

EXERCISE: YOUR OWN MOM

Recently I sent out a questionnaire on this topic to women all over the country as a way to get information directly from moms and daughters. The responses were illuminating in terms of the lessons passed on from mother to daughter. All questionnaires were done in confidence and neither mom nor daughter shared their responses with each other. I asked the following three questions:

1. Describe your memories of the relationship with your mother at the following times:

   Childhood (ages 6–12)

   Adolescence (ages 13–18)

   Adulthood (over 18)

2. Describe specifically what you will do (or are trying to do) differently with your daughter from what your mom did with you. Why?

3. Describe three key outcomes or coping skills you obtained from your relationship with your mother.

   Here's how one woman responded:

   Until I reached the age of thirteen, I honestly felt my mom could do no wrong. She taught me everything from how to sing to how to fold napkins into cool shapes. She always knew what was going on in my life, my friends, my school schedule, even my dreams of being the first lady president. She supported me and loved me no matter what.

   When I got to be thirteen, something changed. I thought it was me, but now I realize it was her. At the time, it felt like she turned on me, and I was really confused. Suddenly, she wasn't as interested in my life or my friends. Those years were lonely for me. Much later, I found out that my dad was having an affair at the office, which is why mom was so miserable.

I wish she had been able to tell me what was going on. Maybe not all the gory details, but at least it would have been better than always being kept in the dark about her life and her feelings.

I vowed never to do this to my daughter, who is now eight, and I don't think I have. Still, sometimes I wonder if I share too much with her and treat her too much like a buddy instead of a daughter. Even if it's wrong, I guess it's better than the way I had it with my mom.

I did learn some key coping skills from my mom, like how to stop myself from crying too much by distracting myself with something mindless like reading a gossip magazine or watching a TV talk show. I also learned that a glass of wine and soft music can be soothing when I'm upset.

Now that you've completed this exercise on how you were mothered, I'm going to ask you to dig a little deeper.

EXERCISE: YOUR OWN TEN COMMANDMENTS

In your journal, write down the top ten messages you received from your mother—either overtly or more subtly through her behavior. These could range from the mundane to the profound, and offer both positive or negative ideas. For example:

- Always wear clean underwear.

- Make your bed every morning.

- Thank-you notes should be sent within a week of receiving gifts.

- A handsome man cannot be trusted.

- Never have sex until you're married.

- It's OK to scream at the waiter when it takes a long time for your food to arrive.

Then turn to a clean page in your journal. Honestly consider what messages your daughter has learned from you, either overtly or subtly, whether positive or negative. After you've made both lists, compare them. Ask yourself the following:

Am I teaching (or have I taught) my daughter the messages I learned from my own mother? Do I want to be teaching my daughter these messages?

Looking through the lists as a whole, are there any general themes occurring—such as honesty, trust, or love?

Is some kind of legacy emerging, a specific lesson that is being passed on through the generations?

No matter what your relationship is like with your daughter at this moment—whether you believe she adores you or can't stand the sight of you—she is still your daughter and she feels connected to you. (Remember Truth #1? Mothers and daughters want the same things: love, understanding, and respect.) Certainly you understand this; otherwise you wouldn't be taking this journey with me. The up-front work you've done speaks volumes about just how committed you are to improving the relationship you have with her. You have already achieved great success. You have internalized the Four Truths about mothers and daughters and have worked hard to be a strong role model for your daughter. You are a person who knows what she's about and continues to seek balance in her life. Your customized tool kit will help. Even on those days when you're not feeling at the top of your game—and we all experience those kinds of days—getting back to a position of strength, balance, and clarity will be easier now that you have the tools to do so. That resilience will serve you well as we shift our focus from you to your daughter.

After spending so much time on yourself, it may seem odd that I'm asking you to put that self aside. Yet it's the next step in this process. Let's begin by taking a look at your daughter's S.W.E.E.P. As you know, the ultimate goal of S.W.E.E.P. is to achieve balance in your life. By S.W.E.E.P.ing your daughter, you will be clued in to her interior life. Understanding her S.W.E.E.P. will give you both valuable information about how the two of you affect each other's key areas with regard to strengths and weaknesses. In turn, the stage will be set for the best potential outcome of the Chair Strategy.

EXERCISE: S.W.E.E.P. YOUR DAUGHTER

If your daughter is under the age of ten or so, this exercise is something you should do for her and help her make adjustments. If your daughter is ten or older, this is something you can do together. (The asterisks indicate new questions pertaining to school-age children that you must consider on her behalf.) And if your daughter is an adult, S.W.E.E.P. is a tool she should have—please share this exercise with her!

In your journal, record your responses (and suggest to your adult daughter that she record hers).

Sleep

How much sleep do you get on an average night?

What one word best describes the way you feel in the morning when you wake up?

Do you sleepwalk? Sleeptalk?

Do you hit someone or objects during your sleep?

Do you cry out or scream?

Do you dream when asleep?

Do you remember your dreams?

Do your dreams feel like they're part of your day?

Are they happy? Scary?

Is there a common theme to your dreams (such as being lost in a crowd)?

Do you look forward to bedtime?

Do you have a routine before bed? If so, what is it? Does the routine involve another member of your family?

Do you need to read before falling asleep? Watch TV?

Do you get ready for bed at the same time each night?

Are you the first or the last one in your house to get ready for bed?

Are you the first or the last one up each morning?

Do you nap?

What clothing do you sleep in? Do you have a reason for that choice?

Is your bed comfortable? If you sleep with someone else, is the bed the right size for the two of you? Is it a place you look forward to being in at the end of a day?

When you walk into your bedroom, do you feel a sense of comfort?

Do you love your sheets and pillows?

As you sleep, do you hear disturbing noises or distractions—traffic, television, snoring?

Is the temperature comfortable in the room where you sleep?

Is the room you sleep in used for anything else, such as work or watching television?

*Is she sleeping the required amount of time for her age group?

*Does she have a sleep routine for every night?

*If napping, how is that schedule working?

*Is she happy to go to sleep at night?

*Is she afraid of sleeping or being in her bedroom?

*What's her favorite part of getting ready for bed?

*What would she change about her bedtime—either the time or any routine surrounding it?

*Does she have a favorite bedtime story? Why or why not?

*Does she feel warm and cozy in her bed?

Work (*School)

What are your job duties? Are they what you thought you were hired to do?

Is your work fulfilling? Do you see tangible results from your work? How do you feel about those results?

What are your goals at work?

Are you achieving those goals?

Do you view your current work as a stepping-stone to something else or as the place you really want to be? If it is a stepping-stone, what are you working toward?

Do you have friends at work? If so, do you have a chance to socialize or eat lunch together?

Are you confined in a cubicle all day?

Do you have windows in your office?

Is there tension at work between you and others?

How is your relationship with your boss? With your subordinates?

Do you socialize with your co-workers outside the office?

Do your family issues seep into your time at work? Does this bring stress?

Does your work financially reward you? If so, are you satisfied with that compensation?

How did you get your job (e.g., educational training, word of mouth, via a relative or friend)?

Do you feel appreciated and respected at work? If not, what are some examples?

Do you work at more than one job outside of the home?

If you are a stay-at-home mom, how many hours a week are spent on that work?

*Does she do well in school socially? Academically? Behaviorally?

*Does she have any struggles or behavioral issues worth noting?

*How are her study habits?

*Does she enjoy school? What kind of mood is she in when she comes home?

*Do you reach out to her teachers and know what's going on in class?

*Do you know whom she hangs out with at school?

*Does she like her school?

*Does she enjoy her teachers?

*What's her favorite subject?

*What is the most difficult detail about school for her?

*Does she eat her lunch with her friends at school?

*What would she change about her time spent at school?

Eating

Do you eat regularly throughout the day? At what times?

What do you eat?

Do you enjoy eating?

Do you have a favorite food or type of food? How often do you get to eat it?

What prompts you to eat (hunger, headache, time of day)?

Do you skip meals? Are you constantly dieting? Do you go without eating for an extended period of time?

Do you get irritable when you don't eat?

Do you overeat? Do you binge then purge? Do you eat or eat more when you are emotional (anxious, sad, happy, etc.)?

Do you think food is vital to maintain good health? Do you think it's a mechanism for survival?

With whom do you eat?

Which types of eating experiences do you enjoy: with family, alone, with friends, at home, in a restaurant, at someone else's home?

What role do you play in your family's eating (planning, shopping, cooking, cleaning up, coordinating schedules)?

Do you eat with your family at least three times a week?

Do you and your family talk with one another when you eat? If so, is it chitchat or deeper conversation? What are some of the topics you talk about?

Do you feel a real connection to your family during mealtime?

What room do you generally eat in?

Is the TV on during mealtime?

Are there any other activities going on around you during mealtime?

*Does she eat with friends at school?

*Does she bring or buy lunch at school? If buying, do you know what she's eating?

*What's her favorite food? How often does she eat it?

*What's the food she dislikes the most?

*What's her favorite restaurant and why?

*Does she enjoy cooking or baking? What types of food?

*Does she ever feel sick, too full, or still hungry after she eats? If so, why?

Emotional Expression of Self

Are you involved in intimate relationships, both sexual and emotional?

What is fulfilling in those relationships?

What is not fulfilling in those relationships?

Do you have sexual desire?

How do you handle feelings of rage, sadness, fear, happiness, disappointment, and frustration?

Do you know intellectually when you are feeling any of these emotions?

Are your heart and head connected during that process?

How do you express these feelings to others?

Do you cry, laugh, and smile?

Are you able to control these emotions or do they get out of hand?

*Does she throw tantrums?

*Is she typically frustrated?

*Is she easy to get along with?

*Does she text, e-mail, and make phone calls? If so, how much?

*How does she show her anger?

*How does she show happiness?

*What makes her smile? Happy? Sad? Scared? Anxious?

Play

Describe what is fun for you to do.

How often do you have fun?

Have the activities you consider to be fun changed over the years?

Is your mom the only person you have fun with?

Did you pick these activities or hobbies or did they pick you (e.g., school volunteer duties)?

Do you share these hobbies/activities with your friends? Or do you do them alone? Do you have a preference?

Do you exercise? If so, how often and what type of exercise do you do?

Is there any exercise you would like to be doing but can't seem to find the time for?

Do you see your friends in a social setting?

Do you spend any alone time caring for yourself (such as getting a massage, preparing a special meal, reading a book for pleasure)?

*Does she have playdates? Do the kids call her for subsequent dates?

*Does she go to other people's home to play? Does she have her friends over?

*Does she have extracurricular activities?

*Is she part of any social groups?

*Does she have any favorite activities she does alone?

*What does she spend her time doing when she is with friends?

*Does she have friends from school and the neighborhood?

EXERCISE: S.W.E.E.P. FOLLOW-UP FOR DAUGHTER

Now that you (and your daughter) have considered the previous questions and jotted down your responses, please refer back to pages 50–53). Again, remember, this is not a one-time exercise but an ongoing process.

Your Tool Kit

1. Strength: Don't forget the four truths
2. Balance: S.W.E.E.P. yourself
3. Clarity: Your Daughter, Your Opportunity

. . .

At this moment, mom, you are at a crossroads. I hope that you are ready to move on to the next phase of our journey. Alternatively, you may feel that this process has given you what you need and the next step, which requires more of your attention, is unnecessary. Stay with me, though . . .

I promise you our next focus, the Chair Strategy, will change the relationship you have with your daughter forever. Believe me when I tell you that you have already completed the hard work. You will enjoy the benefits of the Chair Strategy in direct correlation to the up-front work you have already done. So you are way ahead of the game. The honesty and commitment you've given to this process so far will continue to pay off even more. Not just for you, but for your relationship with your daughter.

PART TWO

The Chair
Strategy

A week before I opened the door to my very first private-practice psychiatry office, I realized I had overlooked one important thing . . . furniture! I literally had nothing for my patients to sit on during their sessions. Having spent every last dime on my medical training, I was flat broke. So I went to several secondhand furniture shops in search of that proverbial shrink's couch, hoping to find something cheap. My dream was a wood-framed 1950s-era sofa with thick, comfortable, velvet cushions. But at $399, the couch was not for me. So I settled for two stray wooden chairs left behind from a dining room set. Definitely not the prettiest chairs, but they worked. And though it was very disappointing at the time, it turned out . . . those chairs changed everything.

Getting Started with the Chair Strategy

S EVERAL YEARS AGO, as I waited in my office for a mother and her daughter to arrive for their first session together, I heard a loud noise coming from the hallway. As the sound grew closer, I realized what I was hearing were two angry voices. At that point I heard several people from neighboring offices come out to see what was going on. I knew in my gut it was my four p.m. appointment.

I opened my office door. Two women approached, both red-faced in anger. It was Julie, a sixteen-year-old, and her mom. They looked my way and, without missing a beat, continued their exchange.

Julie: You're a bitch. You know that, right?

Mom: Takes one to know one!

Dr. Sophy: Hi, you must be my four o'clock?

Mom: Yes, doctor.

Julie: Deal with your own crap, Mom. I'm going home!

Julie stormed off.

Mom: Dr. Sophy, welcome to my world.

Dr. Sophy: Please, let's try to get Julie back in . . .

Mom: Let her walk home. I can't stand the sight of her right now!

The first time a mother and daughter have a session in my office together, particularly when that daughter is over the age of ten, there reaches a point when one or both of them get very loud. Sometimes, the exchange can get quite ugly. Some mothers and daughters, like Julie and her mom, walk in already at their boiling point, with the intensity and rage of two fighters in a boxing ring. Those are the times I must remind myself that I am not, nor will I ever be, a referee. That is not my job, though having a whistle around my neck wouldn't be such a bad idea.

Typically, when a mom and daughter initially come to see me, they are there because one or both of them truly feel they are in crisis. Otherwise, they would not be sitting in a psychiatrist's office. The specific issue could be anything from poor homework habits to illicit drug use. In my opinion, though, unless the identified issue is literally a life-or-death situation, it is not a crisis. The unhealthy communication going on between the two of them—in which neither is being respected, much less heard or understood—*that* is the true crisis. And we begin by addressing that crisis.

Now that you have an idea of the initial interaction I observed between Julie and her mother, take a guess what the issue was that brought them in to see me. Turns out, the argument began over the fact that Julie had sent a late-night text message to a male friend. Mom felt it was inappropriate to be texting at that hour, especially to a boy. From there, their relationship had unraveled until the time when I met them.

I'm not saying that text messaging cannot be cause for a heated discussion between a mother and daughter. More important, though, is that the disrespectful communication between them had reached a toxic level. I hope you understand that this kind of interaction was the real crisis.

Of course, my presence may have exacerbated the volume and drama between Julie and her mom, as oftentimes the act of visiting a psychiatrist stirs up added angst. It was their way of both consciously and subconsciously asking me to pick a side. Even the initial noise I heard from the hallway was their way of announcing their personal stake in the session to come. Nothing would have made either of them happier than if I had pointed to the other and proclaimed, "Yes, you are right!" This will never happen, of course. The moment I choose a side, I lose credibility as a neutral third party.

There's another reason why the volume and drama typically increase around me. People in pain want to be reassured that I understand that they're hurting, and they want me to respond with compassion. I don't need, much less want, shouting or other dramatics in order to feel compassion or to gain understanding about why two people are in real pain. What I do need in order to help are clear thoughts delivered with slightly less emotion. Give me that, and we're off and running.

After Julie left, her mom and I walked into my office. After a moment, she pulled herself together. She took a deep breath and sat down. Julie returned and poked her head in.

Julie: Don't fill his head with lies about me.

My first goal in a session such as this is to calm down the participants. The challenge is to somehow get them to lower the volume and extract some of the emotion. This is the only way the two of them can begin to have an objective understanding about how they are communicating. This requires that they trust me—trust that the only side I am on is their collective side so that their crisis can be resolved, trust that I will understand the situation fully, without the emotion. Once I gain their trust, the challenge becomes to help them make sense of their situation, to enlighten them of the other person's pain, and to assure them there is a solution.

How do you convince a mother and daughter that yelling at and blaming each other will achieve the opposite of what they are hoping for? How do you convey to a fuming mom and daughter that there is a solution but first they must acknowledge that each is part of the problem?

Back in the early days of my psychiatric practice, helping my patients understand how they communicated with each other was one of my initial goals. I wanted to help them find a way to visualize what their conflicts looked like. The idea of putting up a mirror on my office wall crossed my mind, yet I knew this would be too overwhelming. What I needed was a three-dimensional visual of some kind to illustrate the volatility or unhealthiness that I saw between them.

There are several real benefits to learning in a concrete style. It is a way to feel as though your hands are on something that is not actually tangible, namely feelings. Having a concrete or visual reminder is a way to more clearly understand your own feelings and to have access to how the other person in that conflict is viewing those feelings. This helps both participants to better understand their personal role in it so they can take responsibility for their part. And it ultimately enables the participants to figure out how to move through that conflict effectively.

Time after time, as I listened and watched mothers and daughters go at it with rage and nastiness, I noticed the natural shifting of their bodies and the slight maneuvering of the chairs on which they were sitting. The more heated and intense the discussion, the more one or both would turn away from the other. In the case of Julie and her mom, when Julie returned to the session, she literally slid the empty chair that had been positioned next to her mother as far away as possible before she sat down. I have also observed the opposite. In a session where understanding, respect, and connection were strong, the patients' chairs and bodies were more directed toward each other. It made complete sense; it is classic body language. The position of two chairs was the perfect visual I needed to help patients see what their emotional conflict looked like.

Those two stray wooden chairs I so loathed essentially became the basis for what I now call the Chair Strategy. I have effectively used this technique with thousands of patients and it will work for you too. Undoubtedly, it will bring you and your daughter to a healthier and more loving place of understanding and respect.

The Chair Strategy: Overview

The Chair Strategy is a strength-based strategy with you, mom, as the designated driver. You will begin by simply observing the way you and your daughter typically communicate, verbally and nonverbally, during times of peace and conflict. Then you will work to improve that communication. The difficult stretches of time between the two of you will not disappear completely, nor should they. These tough times can lead to true growth in your relationship. It is the *damage* that we want to avoid. The Chair Strategy is designed to bring strength, respect, and safety to your communication so that no issue you face will completely derail your relationship.

The Chair Strategy is based on the idea that you are always subconsciously communicating with your daughter in one of three positions, depending on the metaphorical placement of two chairs. They are:

Back-to-Back

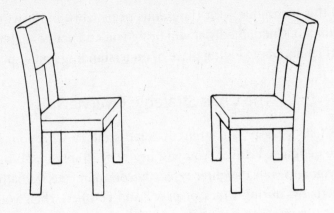

Face-to-Face

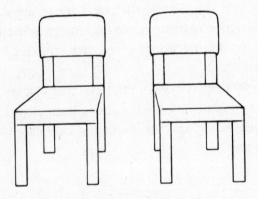

Side-by-Side

Any time you are communicating with your daughter, whether you are literally sitting in two chairs, standing up, on the telephone, texting, e-mailing, in separate rooms, or even on separate continents, that communication can be described by one of these three positions. Now that you have the simple concrete visual in your head, let's take a look at how each position promotes or interferes with your healthy communication with your daughter. I'll first describe each position, and then we'll learn how to enter into conversation with your daughter in the differing positions as well as how to navigate from one to another.

Back-to-Back Position

Mom: Your math homework is so sloppy! I can barely read any of these numbers.

Daughter: Who cares? All the answers are right.

Mom: What do you mean, "who cares?" I care and you should too!

Daughter: Leave me alone. No one asked you to go over it anyway.

Have you ever been in an argument like this with your daughter, when everything she said was disrespectful or confrontational? Or when she felt the same about your responses? Or when neither of you was listening to the other, when the silence smoldered, or there was a complete verbal shutdown?

Welcome to back-to-back, the ultimate in disrespect. Other words associated with this position are:

Angry

Aggressive

Competitive

Malicious

Loud

Shutdown

Antagonistic

Sarcastic

Ignoring

Silent

Of course, sitting in the back-to-back position allows for no eye contact or real connection. This makes resolution impossible. Back-to-back communication is aggressive, loud, and often vicious. At times it may mean that the two of you are not speaking, much less listening to each other at all. Physical and verbal abuse falls under the category of back-to-back. And for some mothers and daughters, this kind of abuse can actually be the result of this consistent positioning.

Even before your daughter could verbally express herself, she asserted her back-to-back position toward you in the form of tantrums. Protesting bedtime, refusing to eat a green vegetable, insisting on buying two toys when you set the limit at one—these are all early forms of this communication style and are to be expected.

As difficult as it is, you should try not to initiate a dialogue with your daughter while in this position. For example, Alexis, a fifteen-year-old high school sophomore, came home and told mom about a classmate who was pregnant. Her mom's response: "That's horrible! Shame on that girl!" This is classic back-to-back behavior. What's so unfortunate is that Alexis's mom was just handed the perfect moment to open a respectful and loving dialogue about an important topic. As previously discussed, mom's reaction to this may have had to do with her own issues. Or it could have simply been the kind of response she'd have on any issue she wasn't ready to face with her daughter. Either way, you can see how the back-to-back position has the potential to be damaging—both in that particular situation and over time.

By the same token, there's a place in your relationship with your daughter for this position as it can be a real eye-opener and can lead to positive growth. If you've ever had a knockdown, drag-out fight and come out the other side, you have already experienced (to some degree) the kind of growth I'm talking about. You've weathered a volatile exchange with your daughter and seen the range and the limits of each other's emotions. Witnessing and experiencing this kind of passion can teach you several points:

1. *How strong your relationship is:* As awful as it may have been between the two of you, you have moved beyond it.

Prolonged Cases of Back-to-Back: Reasons and Consequences

If you find yourself in a prolonged back-to-back position with your daughter, it probably has something to do with your own unmet needs in that area. If you have addressed these unmet needs but still find yourself in this stance with your daughter, it is most likely because she disagrees with your position. In such a case:

- With a younger child, since you are responsible for making so many decisions on her behalf, you can choose to insist or back down and move on. Only you can weigh the pros and cons of this battle. Pick wisely.

- With an older child, it is still up to you to decide whether or not to insist on your position. Consider that this may not be a battle you choose. Sometimes adopting a more flexible position to avoid creating a bad situation is wise. And the respect and support—in the form of flexibility—she gets from you goes a long way.

Remember that when mother and daughter are stuck in the back-to-back position, the damage can be severe. Joining a gang, getting pregnant, using drugs, and committing suicide are some of the extreme ways in which a daughter might choose to deal with the pain of being emotionally disconnected from her mom, the kind of disconnection that comes from being back-to-back with her for much too long.

2. *How strong each one of you is:* Respect the fact that you have a mind of your own, as does your daughter.

3. *How undesirable it can be:* This position may have scared or upset you and will motivate you to try your hardest to stay out of this zone.

These times, hopefully, will be brief, serving more as cathartic venting sessions between mother and daughter rather than a long-term destination.

When you find yourself in a back-to-back position, you have two choices: stay there or figure out a way to get out of the position.

Watch Your Back-to-Back

I was at the park reading when I heard a young voice sweetly ask: "Mommy, will we see horrible bitch here?" I looked up and realized the question came from a four-year-old. Her mom, completely embarrassed, quickly looked around to assess who may have heard this comment, then quieted her daughter. I continued to read, and mom asked: "You heard that, didn't you?"

Dr. Sophy: Yes, no worries, though.

Mom: I'm just so embarrassed. No, more like mortified.

I reassured her again. She sat down next to me on the bench while her daughter played in the sandbox. Mom started to cry, and then just started talking. She explained that the day before, she had gotten into a fender bender in the grocery store parking lot with a woman driving another car. They began arguing over who was at fault and ended up exchanging phone numbers to settle it later. When mom got back in the car, she was upset and began to call the woman a "horrible bitch." At the time she thought she had said it to herself quietly under her breath. Clearly, her four-year-old strapped in the car seat got quite the earful.

I explained to mom that the inappropriate language her child heard should be far less concerning to her than what her daughter observed: mom initiating a hostile back-to-back encounter with a stranger. I make this point to remind you to be mindful of the way you communicate with others. Your daughter is watching.

Your move will be what initiates the shift, especially if your child is young. If your daughter is older and understands the theory behind the strategy, she could also initiate the movement. Generally speaking, though, it is the participant who is more in control of her emotions who will have to lead the way—and that will be you, mom, most of the time.

Face-to-Face Position

Mom: I can't read all of these numbers on your math homework.

Daughter: It's fine. My teacher will be able to figure it out.

Mom: I think it would be better to make some of this a little neater.

Daughter: I think that's a huge waste of time. Besides, I know all the answers are correct.

Mom: It's not just about the answers being correct. Your work really should be neater.

Daughter: It's not that important, Mom, really.

Mom: It is very important. And next year I know the school really cracks down on neatness.

Daughter: Great, then I'll get neater next year.

Mom: Come on, I'll help you redo some of this.

Daughter: OK, I get it.

Face-to-face is the ideal position for working through heated conflicts and serious disagreements with your daughter. If back-to-back is the most difficult way to communicate, face-to-face is the least difficult and most appropriate and respectful way to convey this same passion. Visually, of course, it naturally allows for:

- Eye contact

- Active listening

- Proximity for touch

- Emotional expression

- Body language

These elements bring respect and true connection to the face-to-face position. You and your daughter can be open to each other's ideas and able to hear them, even though they are contrary to your own. You are able to reassure one another, even when you're in disagreement. When you're in the face-to-face position, the language can certainly be strong as you try to sway the other person's opinion, but it remains respectful. People generally describe this stance using the following terms:

Respectful

Intense

Open

Exciting

Passionate

Powerful

Collaborative

It is very difficult for a relationship to sustain such intensity, though, even when that intensity is respectful as it is in the face-to-face position. It is exhausting, for one thing, to be around someone who is constantly expressing herself passionately and in your face. The intensity can feel aggressive to the receiver. Over time, this passion can wear down tolerance and wear out its welcome. This is why face-to-face is an unrealistic place to be forever with your daughter. Nonetheless, the passion it allows can be emotionally satisfying. Face-to-face is the only way to get two people with passionate opinions to truly respect one another.

Imagine if you were always in a face-to-face with your daughter about the fact that her bedroom was messy. At some point you will realize that either you have to accept her messy ways or come up with another solution that works for both of you. (These are both side-by-side solutions, which will be discussed next.) A constant in-your-face dialogue about the messy room will get tiring for both of you. Work through the issue in a face-to-face position, and after you've been respectfully heard, agree to move on. Once you have done this, try to stick to the agreed-upon solution so you don't have to return to the face-to-face on the same issue.

One of my patients was having a difficult time with her seven-year-old daughter, Sally, who received a dollhouse for Christmas and wanted to bring it along everywhere. She asked to bring it to a restaurant one night to play with during dinner. Mom's initial reaction was: "I said no! How many times do I have to tell you this is a stay-at-home toy!" Mom's back-to-back position sent Sally into such a tailspin, the entire family ended up staying home that night and eating leftovers. When mom told me this, I pointed out what might have happened if she had approached this situation in a face-to-face position:

Sally: Mommy, can I pleeeeease bring the dollhouse out to dinner tonight?

Mom: I know how much you love that dollhouse, but it's simply not the kind of toy we can bring to dinner with us.

Sally: Why? I really want to! Pleeeeeeeeeeeeaaaase!

Mom: It's simply too big to bring with us. When we come home from dinner, you can play with it, OK?

Sally: It will be time for bed, it will be too late!

Mom: You're right, it will be late, Sally. Tell you what, you have two choices. You can bring one of the small dolls and a piece of furniture to play with at dinner or, when we get home, you can stay up an extra ten minutes to play with your dollhouse.

Sally: Yes! I will play with it when we got home. Thanks, Mommy!

Though mom understood the idea of face-to-face, she insisted that because this was such a recurring issue, she simply didn't feel this would work. Though I agreed that it might take a bit more back-and-forth to resolve the issue, I was able to help her understand that the only position in which to approach the matter was face-to-face. In fact, this is the perfect place to strive toward when you're coming from a back-to-back position. The challenge there is to retain the intensity and passion of the back-to-back posture, add in respect, and lose the volatility and meanness. Then I gave this mom some techniques to help her move toward the next position: side-by-side. Later in this chapter, we'll discuss those techniques too.

The Challenge of Face-to-Face

One of the greatest challenges of the face-to-face position is to continue maintaining this stance even when your opinion—though respected by the other participant—is not being embraced by her. Keep in mind that this position is the only way you and your daughter can successfully work through a difficult issue. As long as you are being heard and respected and are offering the same, what more can you ask?

If you continue to feel frustrated, don't give up and choose disengagement. This will only send you to the back-to-back position.

Stick with it.

Side-by-Side Position

Mom: You did a great a job on this math homework. I wasn't sure, though, is this a seven or a two?

Daughter: It's a two.

Mom: OK, good. Maybe you should just make that line a tad darker. What about that one, seven or two?

Daughter: I think it's a two; yeah, it's a two.

Mom: Maybe we should clean this up a bit, what do you think?

Daughter: Nah, the teacher should be able to read it.

Mom: Yeah, though it's probably not a bad idea to clean up some of these numbers. Just in case. I'll sit with you while you do it.

Daughter: Sure, why not?

As this scenario illustrates, in the side-by-side position, mother and daughter are supportive of one another but open to disagreement. They are looking in the same direction and from virtually the same place, though they are not necessarily seeing the same view. Mom's and daughter's chairs may be facing the same way; however, that does not guarantee they have the same viewpoint. This position enables both of them to explain their perspectives in a neutral way and then to work toward a resolution—even if the resolution is to disagree. It is the preferred place for just about any communication with your daughter and the ideal place to spend most of your time. It allows you both to stand firm in your observations, opinions, ideas, and choices while at the same time showing respect for each other. It's most commonly described with terms like:

Accepting

Understanding

Peaceful

Comfortable

Tranquil

Collaborative

Neutral

Getting to a side-by-side position is a process. Say your sixteen-year-old daughter has a new boyfriend. Instinct tells you he's a bit of a player and at some point he'll break her heart. You listen to your daughter talk about how sweet he is to her, which you yourself have witnessed on occasion. Still, there's just something you don't like about this guy. But at sixteen your daughter is allowed to date and you trust her. So the two of you reach an agreement on the ground rules: only one date night on a weekend, no phone calls after ten p.m. on school nights, and no breaking curfew. Though your opinion of him hasn't changed, you've accepted that this is whom your daughter is dating right now. Daughter has her boyfriend and her boundaries, and mom keeps a watchful but respectful eye.

Even though you and your daughter have come to a resolution, it is only natural that residual feelings may exist. The trick is not to let those feelings lead you to open up the discussion again once you've reached an understanding. It's very important to ensure trust and safety in your relationship. In this case, mom has made her opinion about her daughter's boyfriend clear, and that opinion hasn't changed. What has changed is the way mom handles the situation. Rather than trying to undermine the relationship (a classic back-to-back position), she has allowed the two of them to continue dating as long as her daughter follows certain rules to which she has agreed. This is a working side-by-side position.

Based on its neutral feel, sometimes mothers think of the side-by-side position as the default stance or an easy way out. But make no mistake, side-by-side has to be earned. And it is never wise to

Don't Be Afraid to Give Your Daughter Freedom

In the previous story, mom wasn't crazy about the guy her daughter was dating and would have preferred she didn't see him at all. Because mom took a side-by-side position and allowed daughter to experience this relationship within certain limits, daughter may very well find out that this young man is not right for her after all. But it is far better for the daughter to come to this realization on her own than the alternative. If mom had approached this issue in a back-to-back position and laid down the law, her daughter wouldn't have felt respected. And just to spite her mother, she may have gone even further by secretly dating him. This could lead to even more trouble.

choose this position as the path of least resistance, to avoid conflict, to save time, or as a temporary way to avoid a battle. (Unless, of course, the disagreement is about something minor, like whether to have Chinese or Italian food for dinner. You have to pick your battles.) This kind of shortcut is actually counterproductive. It robs you of the chance to experience the work that the Chair Strategy's ultimate success is dependent upon.

Certainly, one of the short-term goals of the Chair Strategy is to work through conflict. But the ultimate goal is to devise an ongoing, healthy, and effective means of communication between you and your daughter. The more shared history you have of successfully working out conflicts, the stronger the bond between you. Choosing the side-by-side position to avoid confrontation may seem to serve you in the short-term, but really it cheats you both out of a piece of that history. It also prevents you from exercising the very muscles that this strategy intends for you to strengthen. Working through conflict in a face-to-face position will bring you closer to your ultimate goal of connection.

Side-by-Side: The Ideal

If you are in a side-by-side position, you have successfully worked through a conflict together with honesty, understanding, and respect. You have been open to each other and maybe even learned something new in the process. The more you and your daughter manage to find your way here, the more safety and trust you are building into your relationship. You can never have enough of that.

Understandably, you may be tempted to fall back on the more neutral side-by-side position just to keep the peace, but don't do this when dealing with a major issue or even the issues that will have a recurrent place in your lives, such as homework, dating, and house rules. It may temporarily placate the two of you and even make you feel as if the problem has been resolved, but the real issue you avoided will pop up again. And when it does, it will be even harder to deal with since you've approached the conversation from a dishonest stance, based not on your true perspective but rather on your desire to make peace.

The good news is that the more time you spend in the face-to-face position working your issues out, the more practice you will have in using this approach, and the easier it will become to transition more quickly to the side-by-side position.

Once Upon Two Chairs

One of the questions I often get asked about the Chair Strategy is: At what point in the relationship between mother and daughter can a chair position even be identified? The short answer is: the day your baby girl was born! At that point your chairs were naturally positioned in a side-by-side position. The two of you were in total synch; your identities were clear. She was a newborn; you were her mom and caregiver. During these early days, your healthy baby girl slept, ate, and did all the things she was supposed to do. And you responded in kind by doing whatever you could to meet those needs. The two of you saw things differently, yet were collaborative and looking in the same direction. A smooth side-by-side. Let's take a look, though, at how fragile a position it can be.

Carla and her husband had an extremely difficult time conceiving a child. After ten years of fertility treatments—and five miscarriages—forty-year-old Carla gave birth to daughter Angie. When Carla first came to see me, she was highly anxious and extremely worried about Angie, who was now eight years old and having trouble in second grade. Angie's schoolwork, once quite strong, was now below par. Neither of them was sleeping well, and the two of them argued nonstop about everything, from Angie's rapidly deteriorating study habits to how she dressed and when she went to bed.

The profound disappointment that Carla was feeling at that initial visit reminded her of so many other disappointments she had felt throughout Angie's short life. Carla spoke with resentment about the expectations she had had during her pregnancy, how she'd imagined everything would be perfect once her baby arrived. When Angie was born, Carla was over the moon. In the hospital Carla spent hours staring at Angie, wouldn't let anyone else change her diaper, and in particular loved breast-feeding her. In her mind it was the only way to bond with her baby. And having been through the long, painful journey of infertility, Carla was determined to do everything herself and in her way.

The morning they were going home, Carla's doctor told her that because her breast milk wasn't coming in fast enough, she'd have to supplement with formula feedings. Carla went ballistic, insisted the doctor was wrong, and rejected the idea of using formula. She adamantly believed that breast-feeding was the only way she could truly bond with her baby.

Carla: Can you believe he would tell me such a horrible thing?

Dr. Sophy: Tell me why it was such a horrible thing.

Carla: You're kidding, right? Please tell me you're kidding, Dr. Sophy.

Dr. Sophy: I'm not kidding, Carla. Please explain it to me.

Carla: I dreamed about breast-feeding, and he took that away from me!

Dr. Sophy: So what happened then?

Carla: I freaked out. I screamed, I cried.

Dr. Sophy: Where was Angie at this point?

Carla: Right next to me, screaming and crying too. Angie probably didn't want formula either and was letting me know in her own way.

There was a pause.

Dr. Sophy: Could it be Angie was crying because she was hungry or even scared that you were upset?

Carla: I don't remember exactly, but I doubt it. All I remember is how upset I was.

After only three days together, Carla and Angie's chairs were no longer side-by-side. They had rapidly moved into a back-to-back position.

It is understandable, of course, that Carla would be upset. She had worked so hard to have a baby and had long anticipated, even fantasized about, breast-feeding her newborn. She was experiencing a true loss. If Carla had done the kind of up-front work you have done, however, she might have had a different reaction. When told she'd need to give her daughter some formula, Carla would have been able to separate her own needs (desire to breast-feed) from her child's (nourishment). She could then shift her focus to the real issue, which was that her newborn baby needed more milk. Despite Carla's desire, the reality is that a baby will thrive on formula, as we all know. Baby Angie was most likely crying out of both hunger and fear. Unfortunately, Carla made it about Carla.

Of course, this single event was not the reason why Carla and Angie were stuck in a back-to-back position eight years later. I do believe, though, that the way a mom handles conflicts that arise, even when her child is a newborn, can set a precedent for how she handles issues that come up later on. In our first session together it became clear that Carla's needs continued to take priority, something of which she was totally unaware. At just about every developmental milestone, she would compare Angie to other young girls her age and, in Carla's mind, Angie always fell short. "I just thought she'd be different," she kept saying. Carla told me that her daughter was not "a girlie girl," but still mom insisted she wear dresses and carry a little purse. Again, this was about Carla and, in this case, her need to have that stereotypical girl she had dreamed about. After years of Carla leaning on Angie, of trying to sculpt her into a different creature, Angie finally started pushing back. This was when Carla came to see me.

Carla and Angie's back-to-back relationship may seem extreme, but it certainly highlights the importance of the way you communicate and, specifically, the position you take. It makes a difference and it has consequences, significant ones. It bears repeating that most of the time when mothers and daughters are situated in the back-to-back position, it is because mom's needs got in the way.

No matter what age your daughter is at this point, your chairs can be moved. If your daughter is still a baby or even a toddler, obviously your chairs, no matter what position they are in, haven't been there very long. Moving them should seem almost simple at this point. If your daughter is an adolescent, your relationship may be contentious simply due to her hormones. In that case, moving your chairs is definitely more of a challenge, but still possible.

If your daughter is an adult, you may feel that your chairs have been cemented into one of these positions. If that position is side-by-side, don't be so sure that nothing can rearrange the chairs. It happens, typically because of some major life event, such as your daughter getting pregnant, divorced, fired, or reaching menopause. If you feel the chairs with your adult daughter are cemented in a back-to-back stance, pick up the phone. A simple call from your new vantage point could make a big difference.

It stuns me when a mother who has been locked into a back-to-back position with her adult daughter tells me she can't try anymore. Giving up is not an option, ever! There is no such thing as reaching out to your daughter *too* much, no matter her age. Do not let fear of rejection or humiliation stop you from pursuing a connection with your daughter. She is worth it. And most important, at the very core, mothers and daughters do want the same things: love, understanding, and respect.

If this is your first attempt to call her after a deadlocked back-to-back stance, try the following conversation starters:

- I love you, you know that?

- It's time to move forward.

- We need to heal.

- Let's not do this anymore.

- It's time for us to reconnect.

- Do you forgive me? I forgive you.

Make sure your words (and feelings) reflect the *us* or the *her*, rather than *you* or *I*.

Finally, I want to remind you how quickly issues can come up between you and your daughter. As the designated driver of the Chair Strategy, you must be ready and equipped to navigate these conflicts so that communication stays healthy and effective, no matter how your chairs are positioned.

Understanding the Strategy

Before we discuss how to implement the Chair Strategy, let's review some key points:

- The Chair Strategy doesn't come into play for a particular *issue* you need to address; rather, it is there to improve the *way* you are communicating. This is an important distinction. There will always be differences that arise, and the Chair Strategy provides a framework within which to work them out.

- Regardless of the path the conflict takes—whether the two of you stay in the face-to-face position or go back-to-back several times before reaching the side-by-side stance, it is never about winning. The goal is to work through conflict and come out the other side with your love and respect for one another intact. In this way, the Chair Strategy essentially crowns you both winners.

- Positioning yourself face-to-face at the start of any mother-daughter interaction, particularly one that you anticipate is going to be difficult, is a wise move. The more consistently you can do this, the more your daughter will feel safe to follow you there. Over time, she will start to trust in your openness and respect and will reciprocate more freely.

- Expect to be in the back-to-back position at some point. The real issue is how long you stay there.

- It helps to remain flexible. During those times when you are deadlocked in a back-to-back stance, it is up to you as the navigator to do whatever you can to transition out. I'm not talking about being a pushover but about taking charge of a bad back-to-back situation. Think of it this way: If you and your daughter were literally stuck in a huge mound of mud, you would try various maneuvers to pull her out, and you wouldn't quit until you succeeded.

Drama: A Conflict Derailed

Sometimes an argument between a mother and daughter takes on a life of its own and becomes about something unrelated to the true issue. This happens when mom and daughter are overcome with emotion and, rather than using that intensity to work through the issue, are derailed by emotion and fall back into counter-productive patterns. In the example below, rather than discuss the issue on the table—nutrition—mom and daughter push each other's buttons and become more focused on the emotion.

A fourteen-year-old girl quietly places a box of Froot Loops into the basket while her mom's back is turned at the grocery store. Too late, though—she's caught.

Mom: Hey, hey . . . please put that back. We agreed, no Froot Loops.

Daughter: C'mon, it's the small box.

Mom: I said no. There's just too much sugar in there.

Daughter: You're unreasonable.

Mom: No, honey, I'm thoughtful. I care about your health.

Daughter rolls her eyes.

Mom: Sure you want to make that face at me?

Daughter: What face?

Daughter rolls her eyes again.

Mom: OK, stop it! It is rude and ugly!

Daughter: Stop what?

Mom: You're a spoiled brat, you know that?

Daughter: You are totally out of control!

And they're off and running . . .
Stay focused on the issues.

- Positioning can be contagious. If you approach your daughter in a back-to-back position, chances are, you'll get that in return. By the same token, if you approach her face-to-face, she may very well respond in kind. Remember, the two of you speak the same language. Let it work for you.

- No amount of movement is considered too small. Sometimes baby steps are what it takes to begin. Any movement toward a face-to-face or side-by-side position should be viewed as positive—and will maybe even elicit a smile.

- The Chair Strategy is an investment in your future with your daughter. Each time the two of you work through a conflict and end in the side-by-side position, you will both feel secure in the relationship. This strengthens the trust you both have so that the next time an issue comes up you will be able to handle it. These "deposits" of good will make for a deeper and richer connection.

Now that you understand how the Chair Strategy works, let's talk about how to implement it. There are three steps to the process:

1. Observing and identifying chair positions

2. Changing or moving chair positions to work through conflict

3. Navigating through positions to arrive at a resolution

You will begin by simply observing the way you and your daughter typically communicate, verbally and nonverbally, during times of peace and of conflict (Step One). Then you'll work to change the positions of your chairs (Step Two) as you move through the conflict and finally arrive at a satisfying resolution (Step Three). I'd like to point out that part of the power and charm of the Chair Strategy is that it requires the two of you to work together in fresh and fun ways.

It should be more than clear to you by now that the way you and your daughter communicate is the key to a loving bond.

Therefore, your goal, first and foremost, must always be to ensure that communication is the best possible. The Chair Strategy will teach you how to gain control of yourself during emotionally charged situations so that your bond remains intact and continues to be nurtured. As you use the strategy on an ongoing basis, you will find that these storms will occur with less frequency and certainly with less intensity.

Step One

Observing and Identifying Chair Positions

OVER THE YEARS, I have seen mothers and daughters communicate in many different ways: with eloquent words, tender hugs, and sentimental love letters; with nasty sarcasm, slaps to the face, and threatening hate mail. They can choose to ignore, rebel, or be passive-aggressive with each other. And within these classic ways, there is a range of highs and lows. The commonality here is *emotion*. Women communicate with their hearts more than their heads. This is what makes the mother-daughter pair such a powerful—and volatile—combination.

Observing Your Position

Whether the messages are delivered with words or body language—in person, on the telephone, or via e-mail, texting, or fax—they can be either clear and intentional or unclear and unintentional.

Regardless of these variables, the communication takes place when the two of you are in one of three positions:

Back-to-Back

Face-to-Face

Side-by-Side

The first step of the Chair Strategy is learning to observe and identify these different positions. To be clear, you will be identifying the position you are in *and* the position your daughter is in. These positions can be different. What's important to note here is that you, mom, are the designated driver in this strategy. It is up to you to stand firm in your face-to-face position and to encourage her to do the same. Now that you have an understanding of the three basic positions, this should be a relatively simple task.

In Person

Especially if you and your daughter live under the same roof, you are constantly communicating. Here is a brief look at a couple of hours in what might be your typical day together. Noted are just a few of the potential interactions when you must decide what your message will be and from what position you will deliver it.

It's a Saturday. You and your fourteen-year-old daughter have plans to spend most of the day together. You're driving to your first stop—the bank. Daughter fidgets with the radio to find the station she loves. As she surfs, you hear a passing beat of Barbra Streisand's song "People." You love that song and haven't heard it in years. You ask your daughter to go back to that station. But she just stumbled upon The All American Rejects, and she's not budging. How will you respond and from what position?

You arrive at the bank and park the car. As the two of you are walking toward the entrance, daughter spots her friend about ten feet away. You can't stand that girl, partly because she has a reputation as a troublemaker and partly because her parents didn't invite you to their annual holiday party that everyone is still talking about. Daughter asks if she can hang out with her friend while you go into the bank. Better yet, can she ask her friend to join you two for lunch? How will you respond and from what position?

Lunchtime. It's just the two of you. Turns out, wild child had a dance class (lucky you!). Silently relieved, you tell your daughter to pick a place for lunch. She suggests the greasy spoon whose french fries make your mouth water. Trouble is, you've been dieting all week and you really don't think you can resist those fries. How will you respond and from what position?

In each of these instances, mom has to think on her feet, decide how she is going to react, and deliver the message effectively—essentially choosing a position. For example, in the last scenario mom could choose a face-to-face stance by agreeing to eat at the greasy spoon and asking daughter for help resisting the fries. In this way, daughter gets to choose the place and mom gets some needed help from her daughter with her willpower. It's a win-win situation. They have landed side-by-side simply by accommodating each other.

Even if your daughter does not live under your roof, whether she's away at college or residing with her own family in another city, you are probably in contact with her through phone calls, texting, or e-mailing. This may make it harder for you to determine what positions your chairs are in.

Phone Calls

The telephone is a primary communication device for many mothers and daughters. It can be a great way to connect, but knowing how to identify position during phone conversations can be challenging. Obviously you can't rely on the clues gleaned by facial expression or body language. Aside from the actual words and content of the conversation, you'll have to rely on tone of voice and volume. Poor reception, especially with cell phones, can make it difficult to use even these criteria to make a judgment. One thing is a given, though. The minute you hear disrespect from your daughter, whether in the language she's using or the tone of her voice, you know you are in a back-to-back position. (Of course, this is also the case if one of you hangs up on the other person.)

Talking on the telephone allows for a more uninhibited conversation due to the distance it provides. This "safety" of distance can work for and against better communication. It is easier for some people to express deep and sincere emotion without the actual presence of the other person. On the other hand, it can be too easy to take advantage of this seeming safety to be nasty or harsh and let it all out. And thanks to earpieces and technology like hands-free devices, the freedom that comes from being able to talk on the phone while doing other activities, such as shopping, driving, and exercising, can make it easy to forget the discipline and focus of effective communication. This can bring an unintended intensity to the conversation. Be mindful of this when you're talking on the phone with your daughter, and try to stay in control of your emotions during a potentially volatile phone exchange with her.

In order to determine what position you and your daughter are in while talking on the phone, make note of the following:

- Are you both using respectful or disrespectful language?

- Is your tone sarcastic or agitated? Or loving and calm?

- Are you listening or are you distracted?

- What about the volume? Is it loud or quiet?

Texting and E-Mailing

While we all appreciate the convenience afforded by technology, overall it has been detrimental to the way we communicate. Children and adults everywhere hold on to their BlackBerries or iPhones and respond to the buzzing, ringing, or personalized tune in record time. If they are doing so in the company of others, the focus can shift from the people in their presence to the little devices they are holding. Yet most of these messages, both incoming and outgoing, are shorthand, without emotion, or worse yet, inappropriate. It shortchanges both the giver and the receiver of the communication in that it lacks any human element. There is no sound, facial or vocal expression, or touch. A smiley face emoticon does not convey the same feeling as a big hug.

Another drawback of this type of communication is the lack of tone. The same words can have different meanings depending on how they're delivered. "You sure know how to make people happy" can be a lovely compliment or a wry insult depending on the intonation. Texts and e-mails eliminate this context so all you have to go on are your own mood and your best guess as to what the other person actually means.

Though texting and e-mail are ideal for exchanging information when you are not with someone, I believe that even when intended for closeness, it does not facilitate a true connection. If this is your most common means of communicating with your daughter, know that it will be a bit more challenging to identify each of your positions.

Identifying Your Position

Take some time now to observe and identify those chair positions. The following exercises will help to get you started.

EXERCISE: KEEPING TRACK

Over the course of the next day or two, every time you and your daughter have an interaction, no matter how brief, jot down:

- The basic position you started in

- The basic position your daughter started in

Exercise: Unintended Messages

Unintended messages are the result of communication gone awry. They can be conveyed with words or body language. The verbal version shows up as sarcastic or passive-aggressive comments. For example, daughter comes downstairs in thin cotton pants when it's snowing outside. Mom says: "Are you really going to wear *those* pants today?" Instead, mom could say: "Those pants look fine, but it's cold outside. Maybe you should wear something warmer." (By the way, this works even if you really hate the pants.) The nonverbal version—body language—is often subconscious and involves movements like crossed arms or scowling. Regardless of how they're delivered, the upshot is that these subtle messages can result in mother and daughter being situated in a back-to-back position.

Young children in particular are literal thinkers, so they don't understand the nuances of sarcasm and will certainly not get the joke much less think it's funny. Regardless of the age of the recipient, in the short term, unintended messages are confusing and can lead to your meaning being obscured, resulting in your daughter reacting in unexpected or inappropriate ways—which then causes you to react strongly. Needless to say, over time these kinds of frustrating exchanges will adversely affect the relationship you have with your child.

Your daughter's self-esteem is rooted in how you feel about and react to her. Treat her with love and she will internalize those feelings. Treat her with disrespect and she will start to question her own self-worth, which eventually will land the two of you in a back-to-back position.

- The basic position the interaction ended in

- The emotion you felt both during and after the interaction

If you and your daughter live under the same roof and interact basically 24/7, keep track according to larger or more general time intervals. For example: breakfast time, mid-morning, lunchtime, afternoon, dinnertime, early evening, bedtime.

After each interaction with your daughter, also note:

- Key details about your—and your daughter's—verbal and nonverbal communication (such as eye contact, body language, and tone of voice)

Evaluation

Look through your notes from the above exercise and ask yourself the following:

Is there a position in which I typically initiate interaction?

Is there a position in which my daughter typically initiates interaction?

Is there any kind of pattern throughout the day (such as conflicts occurring in the morning during the rush to get ready for school and work)?

Is there any particular topic that keeps coming up?

If I had to characterize my relationship with my daughter in terms of the three chair positions, which is it?

Have I had any episodes of major back-to-back communication? If so, was it resolved in any way?

Have I experienced any periods of smooth side-by-side communication?

. . .

At this point I hope you've gotten into the habit of noticing how you and your daughter position your chairs. Congratulations! It isn't always easy to step back and coolly analyze a situation, especially if you feel you're under attack by your beloved child. Armed with this knowledge about chair positioning, it's time to move on to the next step: repositioning your chairs as needed to work through conflict.

6

Step Two

Changing Chair Positions to Move through Conflict

T HE CHAIR STRATEGY has become the centerpiece of my treatment with mothers and daughters in both my government work and my private practice. Over the years, it has evolved from the initial visual concept of two chairs into an effective, comprehensive plan that I now use to guide every mother and daughter under my care toward a healthier and more loving connection.

There are several ways for you to use the Chair Strategy. You and your daughter could embrace the Chair Strategy together. If you already have a relationship with your daughter in which communication is typically open and easy, sharing this technique with her can be effective and enjoyable. Together you can experiment and see what works best for you.

Another way is for you to learn about the Chair Strategy on your own. At some point you can introduce your daughter to the concepts, such as when a conflict arises and her participation in the exercises is required. If you choose to do it this way, it's wise to talk about the Chair Strategy before a major conflict arises so you are certain to have her respectful attention. Once she learns about the technique, she may very well be receptive to it. On the other hand, she may not be. If this is the case, don't push, but use this technique for your side of the communication. Never use the Chair Strategy as a manipulative weapon toward your daughter. With a child less than age ten or twelve, depending on the child, the Chair Strategy can be explained by actually using two chairs. It's more effective this way as she is able to see and understand the concepts. This also works for older children and adults who are visual learners.

Regardless of when you choose to tell your daughter about the strategy, I hope you will be open to all of the suggestions laid out here. So, for example, once you understand the techniques of movement, try them all. See what works best for both of you. While the concepts, exercises, and real-life applications presented here are not difficult to understand, they may require you to step out of your emotional comfort zone. The up-front work you already have in place will certainly be a wonderful support for you in that regard.

If you've ever begun an exercise regime, you know that at least in the beginning it can feel as if you're working hard yet not seeing the kind of changes to your body that you'd expected. All those Pilates classes, crunches, and miles of jogging—and still you do not fit into your skinny jeans! This can be frustrating and extremely disappointing and can lead you straight to your freezer to devour a pint of your favorite ice cream. I don't want this to be your path, except maybe for the ice cream part! There's no reason why the Chair Strategy won't work for you. Though it won't happen overnight, it will happen.

How do you measure success in the beginning? Small and simple changes in the interactions you have with your daughter, such as a few more smiles directed your way, an unanticipated laugh between you at dinnertime, an impromptu chat about her current crush. Subtle but powerful, these seemingly trivial issues add up. Over time, you will see how your dedication has strengthened and even reshaped the communication between you and your daughter. Stick with it.

At this point, you should have a pretty good idea of how you and your daughter typically communicate, using the basic positions of the Chair Strategy as a guide. If you had a conflict in the past few days, were you able to see the position that each of you naturally assumed? This awareness is something you should try to maintain, particularly when you sense a conflict brewing. Let me give you an example.

Lisa and her seventeen-year-old daughter, Molly, came to see me after Molly had come home from a sleepover with a tattoo on her ankle. She and her girlfriends had decided it would be cool if they all went and got them together. Molly knew her mother wouldn't approve, so she did her best to hide the tattoo. About a week later, though, Lisa saw it and became furious with her. So furious that she slapped Molly across the face, then grounded her and forbade her to speak to her friends until further notice. Molly begged her mom to forgive her and eventually persuaded her to seek guidance from a professional.

Needless to say, when they initially came to see me, they were firmly positioned back-to-back. As their story unfolded, I learned that Lisa had actually overheard Molly and her friends talking about getting tattoos a few weeks before the sleepover. At that point, Lisa made it clear that getting a tattoo was absolutely unacceptable. When Molly asked why, Lisa's reply was simply, "I said no, Molly. Enough!"

When Lisa overheard the girls' initial conversation about getting tattoos, she greeted it with the equivalent of a hand in the face. Her mind was made up. Even worse, she didn't allow any room for discussion. It wasn't as if Molly had been pestering her mom about it. Lisa took an adamant back-to-back position. There was no attempt on mom's part to listen or to initiate an exchange of opinions. I can't think of any situation a daughter could present to a mom, barring immediate danger, that would warrant this kind of initial response. Mom's attitude fueled Molly's desire for a tattoo and her ultimate decision to get one, yet at the same time her fear of mom's wrath caused her to hide the tattoo. Either way, Lisa's need (no tattoos for Molly under any circumstances) clouded the way she approached this topic. Their relationship suffered the consequences.

Let's imagine we could rewind and play this scenario out differently. After Lisa first heard Molly and her friends talking about tattoos, she could have used a face-to-face approach. The two of them could have had a conversation, even a heated one, but both would have been able to express their feelings safely and the encounter would have been a positive one. Based on mom's strong opposition to tattoos, it's doubtful that even the face-to-face position would have swayed Molly, and most likely she would still want one. Yet the honest, open, and respectful communication on the topic would have yielded a healthier connection based on understanding. Together they could have agreed to disagree and come up with a solution that both would have felt comfortable with, the result being a respectful side-by-side stance. For example, they might have decided to revisit the topic in six months, when Molly turned eighteen, or agreed that Molly would get a henna tattoo first as a trial run.

Depending on what it is that you and your daughter are at odds about, moving your chairs can be relatively simple or more complicated. One of the biggest factors in determining the difficulty of moving out of a position has to do with the particular issues it stirs up for you. For some people, the back-to-back tussle could be over the completion of a homework assignment (maybe mom's mother micromanaged her in this respect). For others, it could be her daughter getting stoned at school (maybe mom was busted and spent a night in jail). If a mom has not done her up-front work, you can see how the very issue on which she lacks clarity or hasn't addressed in her own life would throw her when it comes up in her daughter's life. Ideally, if you have dealt with all of your unmet needs and have truly cleaned house, all topics should be on a relatively level playing field.

In either of these circumstances, it is understandable that a mom's response would be full of emotion. So check your temperature. Be aware of what you are conveying, both verbally and non-verbally. You must remain calm to ensure that your daughter will open up to you so the two of you can communicate effectively. And it is imperative that you listen quietly and respectfully while she does most of the talking, at least initially. Otherwise, you will shut her down from the start. Challenging, yes, but less so now that you are clear about where you stand on many of these topics.

Ideally, then, you begin conversations in a face-to-face position and your daughter follows suit. Realistically, you will find yourself back-to-back in many situations until you get more skilled at this strategy. But what happens when you initiate a face-to-face position and your daughter doesn't follow your lead? This is what learning to move is all about.

Learning to Move

The ideal path during a conflict should be:

Back-to-Back ⟶ *Face-to-Face* ⟶ *Side-to-Side*

Pretend for a moment your eleven-year-old daughter comes home from school on the late side and her clothes smell like cigarettes. When you ask her why, she turns white and says she has no idea. Then you catch a whiff of her breath and it's clear she has definitely been smoking. Your instinct is to yell at her and send her to her room.

The two of you are back-to-back.

You do send her to her room until further notice. But you know this is a perfect opportunity to move your chairs. You must somehow transition from back-to-back to face-to-face so you can talk to her about why you're so upset. What is your next move?

Beginning Move: Unhook and Take a Look

The idea of the first move is to take the emotion out of—or at the very least, reduce the volume of—the moment. That is your sole focus now. I want you to simply unhook from the emotion of the moment so you can take a look and view the situation from a more neutral position. (If your daughter is young, you might think of this step as a time-out.) Either way, the first move is to take a step back to gain some space so you and your daughter can cool down. This period of time can last for a few moments or up to a few weeks. It really depends on the two of you and what has ensued. Unhooking will help you to regroup and find some intellectual clarity. During the take-a-look phase, you should be asking yourself the following questions:

Do I really want to engage in this potentially difficult conversation with my daughter?

What are my motivations for engaging in this discussion?

What is the ideal outcome that I am looking for?

How do I make this discussion more strength-based?

Ways to Unhook

Depending on the age of your daughter and your particular personalities, there are a few different ways to unhook. Below are several techniques that I have found to be effective. All are what I call verbal moves, as they require verbal communication:

1. "Stop! Look at our chairs!"

   In my practice, because mom and daughter are actually sitting in two chairs in my office, I can ask them literally to look at the positioning of their chairs. Once the two of them know the basic positions, it is simple for me to calm them down and redirect the discussion in a healthier and more productive manner. This is also a way to effectively guide them to a new position. When we take a moment to assess their positions on the spot, mother and daughter experience something almost surreal and often quite wonderful. Upon hearing me say, "Stop, look at your chairs!" one or both of the following scenarios typically happen:

- A mother and daughter who are in the midst of battle are suddenly forced to become observers rather than participants in the current dynamic. This typically leads to laughter or tears. Both are good. When a mom and daughter can take pause in a heated discussion to giggle or cry, it's a sign that we're moving in the right direction.

- Mom and daughter know that something inappropriate and disrespectful is happening. There is an instant recognition and acknowledgment that someone isn't playing by the rules we've established. (And with mothers and daughters in therapy, these rules are established up front. We'll discuss them later in the chapter.)

This technique has worked in my practice for girls as young as five. You might try this with your own daughter, though it does require that she have a basic understanding of the Chair Strategy.

2. Stop talking completely.

Literally, stop talking. Be silent. If you and your daughter are in a back-to-back position, the effective amount of time for this silent period is roughly one-third of the time you have been talking in total. So, for example, if you and your daughter were talking for fifteen minutes and then the discussion started to get ugly, the quiet time should last about five minutes.

3. Roll the dice.

For toddlers and tantrums, the dice game is especially use-
ful. Rather than responding to the tantrum with a form
of no, tell your daughter: "Let's take a time-out and play
a game." Most youngsters will welcome the distraction,
particularly when they aren't getting what they want—
for example, to stay up later or watch another TV show.

Here's how it works: Assign a fun activity for each
number on the dice. Roll a dice and whatever the dice
shows, that is the activity you must do. Here's an example
that a mother and her seven-year-old came up with:

Roll a 1: Daughter kisses mom.

Roll a 2: Mom kisses daughter.

Roll a 3: Daughter describes her favorite activity to do
with mom.

Roll a 4: Mom describes her favorite activity to do
with daughter.

Roll a 5: Mom tells daughter one trait she loves
about her.

Roll a 6: Daughter tells mom one trait she loves
about her.

If your daughter is older, it is still up to you to turn
down the heat by suggesting: "Let's take a break for
five minutes and play a game." One mom and her adult
daughter came up with this list:

Roll a 1: Daughter hugs mom.

Roll a 2: Mom hugs daughter.

Roll a 3: Daughter tells mom something she would have
liked her to have done differently in a past conflict.

Roll a 4: Mom gives daughter an example of when she would have liked to have handled issues differently in a past conflict.

Roll a 5: Each tells a joke.

Roll a 6: Make a dinner date, for just the two of you.

As you can see, this is pretty straightforward. Using two dice is another variation and will give you the opportunity to assign more activities. You may even devise a special activity for rolling doubles. The game itself is fun to play, and making the rules can be a pleasant activity for the two of you. The ideal time to come up with your list of activities is when the two of you are not in conflict. It can be a wonderful

Laughter: The Laughter Lifeline

A shared moment of connection based on humor is something that can spontaneously redirect just about any communication. I've seen it time and time again in therapy sessions with mothers and daughters. This kind of connection through humor happens usually one of two ways. First, when a mom and a daughter for a moment—perhaps even a split second—are struck by the ridiculousness of the argument or situation. This occurs randomly sometimes during the unhook phase, and they are able to laugh at themselves. Second, one of them says something that triggers a shared funny memory, such as when daughter is ranting about mom never letting her go out to eat with her friends and it reminds mom of the time the spaghetti fell in her lap.

Sometimes, the laughter lifeline is fleeting and merely serves to extract some of the heat from the argument. Other times, the humor lands and the two of them are taken to a much better position.

bonding experience. I have patients—older daughters and their moms—who still play a variation of this game.

If your daughter knows about the Chair Strategy, she will know about the idea of this game and hopefully will be open to playing it. If she is resistant, I suggest you try to engage her in the activity with as much heart as possible. Let her know how much you care about your relationship with her and that working through the conflict is important to you both.

Before you begin to use any of these techniques, you need to acknowledge that the communication between you and your daughter is not flowing as well as it could. At least in the beginning, mom should be the one to suggest unhooking. If you've discussed some of these techniques during a peaceful time, it will be much easier to begin unhooking mid-conflict. Try saying "Time to unhook" or "Look at our chairs!"

Take a Look

After you've managed to turn down the volume, it's time to analyze the situation. Consider:

- The position of your chair

- The position of your daughter's chair

- If your chairs are back-to-back, you must shift to face-to-face

Now that you've both had a breather, it's time to start working together to move those chairs. Mom will need to make the first movement with her chair. Try to turn face-to-face by literally reaching out to your daughter—giving her a hug or some other physical gesture—and emotionally mirroring that movement. For example, the no-tattoo mom could have said, "Molly, I would like to revisit the tattoo issue. We need to connect better about it and have a different kind of discussion."

Connecting Your Head to Your Heart: Finding the Right Balance

Connecting your head to your heart—an idea discussed in part one—helps you stay present and in the moment with your daughter. There is another component of this connection, however, and this is *balance*. In other words, how much of your response is from your heart and passion, and how much is from your head and reason? The balance of your head and your heart connection informs the way you communicate—therefore the way you naturally position yourself with your daughter. This in turn affects the way she perceives you. This connection becomes easier as you learn to unhook and take a look.

For example: It's early evening the night before your daughter's history final. She's been studying all afternoon—which is good, considering she's barely passing the class. She walks into the kitchen to ask you a favor. In the back of your mind, you know that Green Day is performing that night and a lot of her friends are going. You are anticipating that the favor is to allow her to go to the concert. Your blood is boiling before she even speaks. Your head and your heart are connected, but the balance is 80 percent heart/20 percent head. Your response: "Don't even ask me about that Green Day concert!" (A back-to-back position.)

Suppose that you had unhooked and taken a look? Then your balance could have been closer to 50 percent heart/50 percent head response: "Sure honey, what's the favor?" (A face-to-face position.)

The point is: Try to be aware of the balance of your head and your heart before you communicate with your daughter, particularly on the tough issues.

Resuming Communication:
The Rules of Talking

Now that you've taken the heat out of the back-to-back position and you've had a chance to evaluate, it's time to resume communication. There are four rules at this point that must be established and followed:

1. Respect each other by listening.

2. Do not speak when the other person is speaking.

3. Let the other person finish talking, even if you disagree.

4. Establish a signal (a wink, a wave of the hand) that lets the other person know you would like to talk.

If at any point during this designated talking time, the discussion gets ugly, you must reestablish the rules.

Once the rules have been established, it's time for you and your daughter to decide where to talk.

The Established Signal to Talk

When I mention the rule of establishing a signal to talk, invariably either mom or daughter (though usually daughter) asks, "Dr. Sophy, would it be OK if my signal involves my middle finger?" The other person's response to this question tells me a lot. If both mom and daughter find this humorous and actually take the time to laugh, it is a good indication that these two get it and will be on firmer footing sooner rather than later. When the other person looks upset or has a deadpan reaction, I know my work is cut out for me.

The correct answer to the question, of course, is "No. Obscene gestures are disrespectful." Then I turn my attention to helping them understand their reasons for wanting to use this as a signal.

Location, Location, Location

The surroundings, atmosphere, and site where you and your daughter choose to resolve a back-to-back conflict are important. Sometimes you have no choice and these talks have to take place on the spot in very public places—the mall, the grocery store, a restaurant, or at your daughter's school.

If you and your daughter do have the luxury of time, picking the right location is extremely beneficial. The actual conversation regarding where to have your talk can be fun and quite effective in beginning to move your position. The trick is to embrace the conversation. Don't argue about the *where*; focus instead on the pleasurable idea that you're trying to pick a place to chat. You'd be surprised how this conversation alone can offer great relief for the two of you.

Here are some tips on finding the perfect spot to talk:

- Look for a place or a space where the two of you are comfortable, both emotionally and physically, and a place that you both respect. It could be your home, in a favorite room, at the church, or at your local Starbucks. Wherever you choose to talk, though, it should be with only you and your daughter present—that means no other family members or friends around. For this reason, if you pick a public place, try to make it one that isn't frequented by friends or family, as this will only distract you both.

- Be aware of the intensity of the issue, and if you know one of you feels very strongly, pick a place more comfortable for that person. And try to alternate. Accommodation is key.

- Choose a place outdoors, and even an activity to do while you talk. Having the discussion while you're also engaged in a physical activity—a bike ride, a walk—can take the edge off the aggressive feelings. The activity also serves as a positive distraction.

Children Want You to Talk

On a visit to the *Today* show, I discussed teenage alcohol use and sex and how parents could best guide their children on these crucial issues. Part of the segment was a pretaped interview by Meredith Viera with a group of teenaged boys and girls. What struck me was not the fact that these teenagers were surrounded by or even experimenting with both alcohol and sex; rather, it was that at some point in the interview every teenager mentioned how much they wanted to talk to their parents about these very topics, but didn't know how. They felt shut down by their parents or unable to talk freely. Even worse, they spoke about parents who completely turned their backs on them.

The lesson here: Your daughter desperately wants you to greet her in a face-to-face position. Don't shy away from these topics. The safer your daughter feels now, emotionally, the safer she will feel later on when she wants to come to you to with her concerns. This in turn decreases the frequency of your back-to-back positions. Though it may not always seem like it, she wants to talk about these subjects, and you have nothing to lose in bringing them up.

If you are comfortable with the idea, you may want to share your personal history too. It is an important way for the two of you to connect. In general, the idea that you were once her age and experienced a lot of what she is currently facing is a real comfort to her. You have so much to offer by way of your own past.

The real questions are: How much should you share? When? You know your daughter better than anyone else. You are the expert. There are no hard-and-fast rules, but there are some general guidelines to consider.

- Start early. The sooner you begin sharing your own history with your daughter (in an age-appropriate manner, of course), the better. This will help her form a more complete portrait of you over time.

- Do not lecture. The goal of sharing your history should not be to teach her a lesson, along the lines of, "When I was your age, I wasn't allowed to date, so you can't either!" Rather, the point is to inform her about the way it was for you—"I remember how mad I was when my mom wouldn't let me go out."

By informing her about your past—without being pedantic or passing judgment—you will have a much better chance of earning a coveted spot with her. This is the spot where your actual experience with a specific issue will truly matter to her. She will wonder about (and hopefully ask) what you, that person she's been hearing about for all these years, may have done in the circumstance she is currently facing. Now is the time to share your personal stories, and maybe even some of the juicy details. Don't forget, though, that your daughter is not your friend and you must be respectful and mindful of her age.

The Verbal Challenge

We know that communication is the key component in making a difference between a loving and healthy connection and an adversarial one. Poor or unclear verbal communication can bring you to a back-to-back position—and keep you there. Even a few subtle words can ignite a feud between you and your daughter. Yet it is verbal communication—the very thing that got you into this predicament—that will help steer you out of it. Clear verbal communication is the way to move toward and maintain a healthy position. The good news is that you and your daughter speak the same language (remember Truth #2?), so you should be up to the task.

There are two simple words that will invariably put you into a back-to-back position: *never* and *always*. Because these words are absolutes, they don't allow for any flexibility, which is something you must have for successful communication. These two words are not your friends during conflict, and they are often the reason the conflict started in the first place. As much as possible, try to avoid using them.

Instead of:	Try:
You never clean up after yourself.	Remember last week when you cleaned your room and did a great job? Could you please do that again?
You never get serious about anything.	There are things in life that are your responsibility.
You always act like a baby/child.	There are times in life when it is OK to act silly, but . . .
I always have to be the one to give in.	Well, that doesn't sound fair. How do we change that?

Never Say *Always*; Never Say *Never*

Some moms I've worked with have a hard time giving up *always* and *never* when communicating with their daughters. Here's their reasoning:

- "I'm entitled to use these words. I am the mom."
- "But these words are natural, how can they be wrong?" And my favorite:
- "Why do I [the mom] *always* have to be the one to give things up, and *never* my daughter?"

Sometimes you must initiate the more difficult actions that will shift the chair position. A lot depends on you and your ability to collaborate with your daughter. Starting off with a young child and getting your Chair Strategy technique in place will definitely give you a better relationship in the future. It is surprising to most moms just how effective it can be to eliminate these two words from their vocabulary.

Nonverbal Moves

There are some fights that render it impossible for a mother and daughter to communicate verbally. Sometimes this is because the subject matter is so delicate or embarrassing. And sometimes it's simply because being verbal is not your or your daughter's strong suit. If you find that talking is not working, it's time to try the written move of guided journaling.

Guided journaling can be extremely powerful and effective in transitioning away from a difficult back-to-back position. For some people it provides safety. Here's how it works:

1. You and your daughter write down your own account, whether it is about a particular issue that's brewing between you or the general state of your relationship.

2. At a designated time you take turns reading aloud from your journal, following the Rules of Talking we established earlier.

Guided journaling works for several reasons. First of all, it allows both participants to get out their feelings in the moment (on paper), yet read it when they are calmer and less angry. Both are then able to process the experience differently than when it actually took place. Second, the reader experiences the event without the attached emotions, and the listener hears it when she is feeling less defensive. Third, because of preparation time, both participants have the ability to make sure they've covered all the points and ideas they want to express. Fourth, because participants are not literally in the moment when they hear the other person's account, there is an emotional safety here. Because of this, it is much easier to realize their own part in the conflict as they hear the other's perspective. Finally, it provides an opportunity for some much-needed levity. Sometimes when mothers and daughters hear their own words or their own accounts of the situation, they realize just how ridiculous it sounds. This is another instance when humor can redirect your position.

Though reading the journal can reignite feelings, the circumstances are now different and less tense. There's a security in knowing each will be given the time to have their say. Remember to pick a location that is comfortable for both of you.

If your daughter is reluctant to engage in journaling or in the process in general, continue to encourage her. Based on your expertise as her mother, try whatever you know will work to get her to do something that she is initially reluctant to do. Approach it on her level and keep at it.

Assessing the First Move

Making the first move with your daughter is your responsibility. In times of conflict, it is up to you to initiate the idea of unhooking and taking a look. This is the only way your chairs can start to move, so it is crucial that you get right in there the moment the discussion starts to heat up. If your daughter is over the age of twelve (and aware of the strategy), she will start to unhook herself without being prompted, particularly if the two of you have already had some successes in moving through conflict from:

Back-to-Back → *Face-to-Face* → *Side-to-Side*

After that first verbal or written move, you should take stock and ask yourself these questions:

Did I achieve what I wanted?

Did I use positive and unambiguous words?

Did I respect and follow the Rules of Talking?

Was it worth it?

How would I do it differently next time?

The more you practice these moves, the more skilled you will become at them. As you continue to do so, you will see that you and your daughter will find a natural rhythm and soon your posi-

Are You and Your Daughter Back-to-Back Junkies?

If you and your daughter have a history of back-to-back positioning, including loud and aggressive words and unrestrained venting, you may very well feel a loss of sorts as you begin to embrace the healthier, less toxic position of face-to-face and certainly side-by-side. The emotional high you once got from yelling disrespectfully may have been quite a release. Taking this thrill away leaves you much like any kind of addict going through withdrawal: feeling depressed, jumpy, or anxious. But here's a suggestion: Redirect that negative energy toward something positive, namely an area on your S.W.E.E.P. list that needs to be adjusted. For example, if you don't play enough in your life, take some time to exercise or explore a new hobby. One mother-daughter junkie pair solved their problem by taking an exercise class together. Not only did they redirect their energy, but they also had a lot of fun!

tions will change fluidly. If the heat returns at some point, it's time to go back to unhook and take a look. Before you know it, you will be changing positions so naturally it will be subconscious. This is the goal of the strategy.

Now that you've learned about movement, let's take another look at the hypothetical scenario posed earlier in this chapter about the eleven-year-old who comes home reeking of cigarette smoke. When you question her about it, she lies. Your first instinct is to scream at her and banish her to her room but you know this is a perfect opportunity to move your chairs. Based on what you now know, what would you do?

You are caught off guard by the smell. Your natural reaction is to blurt out, "I smell cigarettes on your breath." When your daughter shuts you out, you realize that a better approach might be to initiate a conversation in a face-to-face position by sharing some information about your past. This is a subtle unhook and take a look. It might go like this:

Mom: I smell cigarettes on your breath.

Daughter: I really don't know why. Mom, stop.

Mom: OK. (Pause) When I was your age, I tried a cigarette. I kinda liked it.

Daughter: Really? You smoked?

Mom: Not really, just every now and then with my friends.

Daughter: Yeah, a lot of girls in my school are starting to try it . . .

In this way you can begin the conversation in a face-to-face position and open up a dialogue.

Now that we've discussed how to move the positions of the chairs, it's time to focus on how to navigate a path toward the resolution of a conflict. This next chapter will illustrate how you can put the three steps of the Chair Strategy to work for you.

Step Three

Navigating through Positions to Arrive at a Resolution

THE FINAL STEP of the Chair Strategy in many ways falls into place naturally as you continue to observe your position and practice (even experiment) with movement. Navigating combines observation and movement and along with your strength, balance, and clarity you and your daughter will begin to arrive at resolutions in a new way.

Donna and Patricia

Several years ago, I got a call from Donna, an anxious mom who was distressed about the way Patricia, her ten-year-old daughter, was dressing. According to Donna, her little girl was looking like a tramp and emulating pop icons like Britney Spears by wearing clothes that were way too tight and revealing for a girl of her age. Mom said she had tried everything. She had explained to Patricia that her getups were sending an inappropriate message and that they were drawing the wrong kind of attention to her. Donna had even tried punishing Patricia, but nothing worked. She wanted her daughter to come in and talk to me. My response, of course, was, "Before I can figure out the issue with your child, I must first spend time with you, the parent." Reluctantly, Donna agreed, and we made a date for the following week.

Mom walked into my office at the appointed hour. She wore a low-cut T-shirt and skintight velour sweatpants, her thong underwear slightly exposed. She sat down and proceeded to tell me she was mystified by her daughter's behavior.

You're probably thinking: "Uh, Donna, did you *look* in the mirror?" The truth is, she probably had. Most likely she signed off on this wardrobe choice and left her house thinking it was OK. Clearly, though, what Donna didn't understand was that her daughter's behavior stemmed directly from her own position as role model. She was communicating to her daughter, in this case through her attire, that this sort of outfit was acceptable and appropriate. She didn't have the tools that you do. Without having done her up-front work, Donna was clueless. She lacked self-awareness, among other things, and was completely oblivious to the messages she was sending to her daughter.

One of the first points that came up in our session was the idea that parenting begins with her, the parent. She immediately got defensive, feeling that my philosophy implied she was somehow responsible for her daughter's clothing choices.

Donna: What are you saying, Dr. Sophy? That it's all my fault, I'm to blame for my daughter dressing like this?

Dr. Sophy: This is not about blame. It is about you, Donna, truly recognizing and believing in your powerful role in the emotional, physical, and spiritual well-being of your daughter. Do you realize how powerful you are?

Donna: I guess, sure. (Pause) So, you're saying it's not my fault, right?

It was so important to her, as it is to so many moms with whom I interact, to be absolved of blame regarding her daughter's inappropriate or unwise choices. And by the way, this mom is an intelligent, respected, and loving woman who simply wanted a black-and-white answer. Fault or no fault. Blame or no blame. But there is no room in this process for blame. There is only room for strength. By the end of the session, Donna understood that the concept of "parenting begins with you" was about all about empowerment.

Next we talked about Donna's S.W.E.E.P. Here is what I discovered:

Sleep: Donna's sleeping had gotten worse over the last several weeks. She was restless and had a recurring dream about being lost somewhere, usually at the airport or in an empty building. She was lucky if she got a good five hours a night. As a result, Donna was exhausted most of the time.

Work: Her work was being a stay-at-home mom. This lifestyle had lost its appeal, and she was starting to feel trapped in the house.

Eating: The family ate together several times a week. Personally, she had good eating habits and watched her weight.

Emotional Expression of Self: Donna and her husband lacked real intimacy and had for some time. She felt this was mainly due to her exhaustion.

Play: Donna tried to meet her best friend at the gym a few days a week. Other than that, she had no real hobbies or interests.

In the course of our conversation, Donna mentioned a few items of note. First, in the previous six months she had lost about ten pounds and had begun to make more of an effort to increase her physical activity. Second, Donna felt as if she was getting old. She wasn't crazy about the fact that she had just celebrated her forty-seventh birthday, and she definitely did not feel sexy anymore. Finally, she repeatedly brought up the issue of her daughter's choice of clothing, which you'll recall is why she initially contacted me. She felt Patricia was getting too much attention for her wardrobe; that boys were eyeing her short skirts and exposed midriff. Patricia was a smart girl and, instead of being known for her academic achievements, mom felt she would become known for her inappropriate dress. This really bothered Donna.

Based on what you've learned so far on our journey together, you can probably see that Donna was projecting a lot of unmet needs onto Patricia. At this point she didn't understand how these needs were getting in the way of her relationship with her daughter. Further, she failed to comprehend that her needs had no place being there in the first place. I asked her to focus on the S.W.E.E.P. and Unmet Needs exercises and to come back in the next week or so with Patricia.

The Following Week

The two of them entered my office, seemingly in a back-to-back position, but that may have been for my benefit. That very morning they had a fight regarding what Patricia was going to wear. Apparently Patricia won that battle; she was dressed like Britney Spears meets Lil' Kim, including a snug T-shirt that barely cleared her belly button. They walked in and sat down. After I informed them about the Rules of Talking, Patricia jumped right in.

Patricia: So, why are we here? (Pause) My mom's crazy, isn't she, Dr. Sophy?

Dr. Sophy: No, your mom is not crazy. Mom, tell her why you're here.

Donna: We're here because you and I keep fighting, and I don't want to fight with you.

Patricia: We fight, Dr. Sophy, because my mom doesn't let me do anything I want. Home is like a prison.

Donna: Prison? Since when does prison serve you three meals a day, make your bed, and drive you where you need to go?

Mom had issues with her daughter. Her resentment was clear.

The volume had escalated, and they had landed in a back-to-back position. I reestablished the Rules of Talking by holding up a sign that said:

1. Respect each other by listening.

2. Do not speak when the other person is speaking.

3. Let the other person finish talking, even if you disagree.

4. Establish a signal (a wink, a wave of the hand) that lets the other person know you would like to talk.

The conversation began again, this time in a face-to-face position. I asked them to move their chairs to face each other. Mom was already there, but daughter joined her after I asked. Mom clearly showed, unknowingly, that she was getting into a natural face-to-face position.

Patricia: Mom, I want to dress this way. All my friends dress this way. It's the style, and I feel really good dressed like this. (Pause) That's all I have to say.

Donna: I understand that you like this way of dressing and that your friends Rona and Madison do it. But you are a little too young, I believe, to be showing so much skin.

Patricia: What does it matter if my skin is showing? I'm not doing anything wrong. It's only skin, everyone has skin. Even you have skin, Mom.

Donna: When I was your age, dressing like this was not acceptable. And I never spoke to my mom like this!

Patricia rolled her eyes.

Patricia: Here we go, another stupid story about when you were a kid. I'm not a kid!

Mom: Don't speak to me that way! I can't listen to this anymore!

Now they were moving into a back-to-back stance once again as mom broke the first rule of talking.

Dr. Sophy: Please, you must respect the Rules of Talking.

They paused a moment, then began yet another attempt at a face-to-face position.

Donna: When I was your age, I never dressed like this. It simply wasn't appropriate dress for a ten-year-old. Please help me to understand.

Patricia: It's just different now, things are different. And I'm not you. (Pause) But I like the way you dress, Mom. It's kind of cool.

Donna: Cool? You think so? You've never said that before.

Patricia: Well, it's the truth.

Donna was elated at this compliment from her daughter; another need of hers was being fulfilled. And it was clear that Patricia viewed her mother as a role model. Donna was starting to see the kind of power she had over her daughter. I took this moment to step in.

Dr. Sophy: Mom, please explain to your daughter why her style seems inappropriate to you.

Donna paused. I could see that things were really starting to click for her, that she was conscious of how her own needs were getting in the way of her communication with her daughter. Mom was visibly upset as she began to talk.

Donna: Patty, here's the thing. You're an individual, I know that. But I am very concerned that the way you dress is not sending the right message to people.

Finally, mom was addressing the issue for the appropriate reasons.

Patricia: What people? What message? I'm totally confused.

Donna: Boys at your school. Dressing like this may make them think that you are different inside than you really are.

I could see that Patricia was listening to her mom's important face-to-face message.

Patricia: It's just clothes, Mom.

Donna: Listen, I have an idea. Why don't we figure out a few things we could do to help make your clothing a bit more appropriate?

Donna looked over at me; I nodded. She was working toward a side-by-side resolution and doing a great job.

Patricia: Like how?

Donna: Well, let's see. How about when you wear a tank top, you also wear a light jacket over it?

Patricia: I don't know.

Donna: What about a sweater?

Patricia: Sweaters are cool. But I don't really have any good ones.

Donna: What about my blue pashmina? You can borrow that.

Patricia: I love that one! Really, I can borrow it?

Donna: Of course.

Patricia: Cool, thanks, Mom.

Mom looked over at me and smiled. The two of them had successfully moved to a side-by-side stance. They had heard each other, spoken respectfully to one another, and found a resolution. At that point, I gave them a few moments to chat in their newfound position. They were mentally going through Mom's closet and figuring out which items Patricia could borrow.

Donna and I continued to work together for a few sessions. The most important realization she had was understanding just how

Note to Mom: You're OK. You Can Do This.

I believe in being kind but direct with my patients. Because of this I am often critical of moms, mostly because I see so many who are only subconsciously aware of the problems they are creating for their daughters in an effort to avoid confronting their own issues. However, I also see many, many moms who are doing their utmost to communicate and interact successfully with their girls. Being a mom is *hard*. I know that. So I am careful to support anything a mom does right, even if it's simply taking the first step in the right direction.

Several years ago, I was asked to visit a home to decide if a particular situation warranted county intervention. There had been several complaints against a twenty-one-year-old mother and her three-year-old daughter from neighbors, citing lots of screaming. When I got to the home, no one was there, so I walked down the street and came upon a neighborhood playground. It was nothing elaborate, just a swing on a tree, a few benches, and a rundown jungle gym.

On the playground, I saw a mom who was clearly having a rough time with her tantrum-throwing toddler. A few other adults and children were around, and it was obvious that the mom was embarrassed. I watched as she tried different tactics unfulfilled she felt in her own life. Donna had worked as a retail salesperson until Patricia was born. She had enjoyed the work but was thrilled when the baby arrived and she was able to quit her job and care for her daughter full time. For a long while now, she had felt less than satisfied with this arrangement but hadn't been able to admit it to anyone—especially herself. Yet she'd been out of the workforce for a decade and was unsure about reentering the job market. Taken together, these details made her believe that she had

to help her daughter calm down. Though nothing seemed to bring mom the outcome she was looking for, she continued to express love and tenderness to her unhappy toddler. With affectionate hugs and calming whispers, it was apparent how much she adored her child and desperately wanted to help her through the tantrum.

I thought to myself: "Wow, somebody needs to tell this mom she's doing a good job." She may not have had all the answers, but she was certainly doing whatever she could and was not being abusive in any manner or putting the child in danger.

After a few minutes the tantrum had run its course and the child, now spent, was leaning against one of the bars of the jungle gym not too far away from mom. I walked over and introduced myself. Then I said, "You know, it looked like you were in a pretty tough situation there, but I think you handled it in the best way anybody could have." She broke down in tears. As it turned out, this was the very mother and daughter that I was assigned to observe in the first place. We sat down together and began to talk. The fact that someone was able to say "good job" to her was the simple but essential encouragement I knew she needed. What I also recognized was that she was already in a back-to-back situation and her child was only a toddler, but she was desperately trying to find a way to communicate face-to-face.

no purpose in life. This is why she had the recurring dreams that left her tossing in her bed night after night. Feeling lost, scared, and fearful for her daughter—but really for herself—she was behaving in ways that made her feel as if she was retaining her youth.

One of the first potential solutions we talked about was the possibility of pursuing some volunteer work. Feeling good about how she spent her time during the day and that she had a reason to get up in the morning would bolster Donna's self-esteem. This would make the time she spent with her daughter that much more satisfying. The idea that she could actually be a better mom by not staying at home surprised her, but she was receptive to the idea and found that spending fifteen hours a week doing work at a shelter caring for victims of domestic violence and their children was extremely rewarding. By the way, Donna did choose to share the Chair Strategy with Patricia, and together they succeeded with it. Patricia especially liked making up her own rules for the Dice Game and even chose her favorite bakery as their destination for the next time they needed a comfortable place to talk.

I want to reiterate that the way mom dressed and her style in general was not the issue. Rather, it was her disconnectedness from her daughter, and more importantly from herself. When I first met Donna, she didn't have a clue as to her own needs at that point. Her lack of clarity would have come through even if she happened to be dressed in a conservatively tailored suit. If she had been aware of her needs and able to remove them from the relationship with her daughter (up-front work), her clothing—even if it was the same—would have seemed different because Donna would have been different on the inside. If she had, for example, a stronger S.W.E.E.P., viewed her daughter as an opportunity, and really embraced her authentic self, dressing that way would have come across differently, with more confidence and more authenticity, sending a message along the lines of: *I am comfortable with who I am, the way I look, and how I act.* That clear message would have been sent to her daughter sooner rather than later and would have made a big difference in their relationship.

Mom's lack of self-awareness began to eat away at her self-esteem, making an already trying time more pronounced. Her decision to dress in a younger style was her subconscious attempt to cover up the real issues, but eventually (of course) they came up.

Baby Steps

The success of the Chair Strategy in any heated situation can certainly be immediate. And once you've successfully navigated a path toward a positive resolution, you will feel more secure within the strategy and it will become easier. My suggestion, if your relationship allows for it, is to start small. Remember that simple and subtle changes over time will contribute in a big way to the cumulative effect of the strategy—a stronger and healthier relationship with your daughter. Take a simple interaction with your daughter and experiment. Here are two situations that can be redirected toward a healthier path if addressed proactively with the Chair Strategy:

1. Your daughter comes home from school with a sour look on her face. Your typical response would be a sarcastic "Someone looks happy." Instead, try a face-to-face approach: "I sense you're not OK" or "Want to sit down with me before you start your homework?"

2. Your divorced daughter calls in a foul mood. She begins to jab at you, insinuating that you are the reason her life fell apart. One innocent remark on your part and she snaps: "You are so stubborn. You know, Michael used to say that to me all the time. You drove him crazy, like you do the rest of us. That's probably why he left." A few minutes later, she starts to rant: "Why do I ever believe anything you say? You're the same person who told me, 'Marry Michael. He's a prince.' I hate my life." Rather than defend yourself or take on the argument, unhook by telling her: "Let me call you back in a few minutes after I make a cup of tea."

The more you practice movement, the easier it gets. Soon, your movements will feel more fluid and you will start to initiate them subconsciously. No matter the age of your daughter, she will start to sense your openness as well as your lack of need to engage in a back-to-back confrontation. The more consistent you are in using this technique, the safer she will feel, and I guarantee your communication will start to move in a more positive direction. In the Chair Strategy, success is measured by movement, no matter how small. Slight changes over time will make a big difference in your relationship. Let's look at another example:

Pam, an extremely anxious single mom, and her sixteen-year-old daughter, Ruby, were fighting over a curfew time for the weekend. Though Pam felt strongly that 11:30 p.m. was appropriate, Ruby was pushing for midnight. Every time Ruby complained that all her friends had midnight as their curfew, Pam's response was: "Ask me if I care." Since I taught these two the Chair Strategy, however, dynamics changed between them. Mom agreed to midnight with a check-in call at 11:30 p.m.

One Saturday night while Ruby was out with friends, Pam had fallen asleep on the entry hall chair, where she always waited for Ruby to come home. She woke up at 11:48 p.m. Ruby wasn't home and had not made a check-in call. Furious, she texted me about what she should do. (Yes, I respond to text messages even at this hour.) In my return text, I reminded her of her ability to be flexible. She had, after all, given her child space. At ten minutes after midnight, as Pam had her phone in hand and was about to dial the police, Ruby walked through the door, apologetic.

Mom: Where the hell were you, and why didn't you call?

Ruby: I am so sorry. My cell battery died, and we got stuck in a parking lot behind a stalled car and, honestly, I didn't know what to do.

Mom: Nobody had a phone you could borrow? Nobody?!

Ruby started to get defensive. At that point, Pam remembered another line in my text to her: *Face-to-face no matter what.*

Mom: You know what, I just love you and I was worried about you.

Ruby: Thanks, Mom, I know that. It was a horrible feeling to be in that car and not be able to call you. I'm going to start carrying a spare battery for my phone.

This slight adjustment in mom's approach started to make a big difference in their relationship. And you will start to see how these adjustments start to add up in the relationship with your daughter.

EXERCISE: PUTTING IT ALL TOGETHER

Now that you, the designated driver, know the rules and guidelines of the Chair Strategy, let's take it for a test drive.

Pick two areas of recurring or prevalent conflict between you and your daughter. The more specific, the better, so you can really put the Chair Strategy to work. After using this technique to the best of your ability, record in your journal how the discussion went by answering the questions below. (Many of my patients keep this kind of written record to refer to as major conflicts arise.)

Issue:

Circumstance:

Questions:

What position did you begin in, and how did you express it?

What position did your daughter take, and how did she express it?

Explain the path you then took, using any positions and techniques used. Write in the form of a list if it's easier.

Technique(s) used:

Resolution:

Here is an example from a mom of a fifteen-year-old:

Issue: Lisa (daughter) spends way too much time on Facebook; it's always a struggle to get her to stop.

Circumstance: Bedtime, 9:30 p.m., she wanted ten more minutes.

Questions:

What position did you begin in, and how did you express it? Face-to-face, kindly asked her to turn off her computer.

What position did your daughter take, and how did she express it? Back-to-back, rude protest. Lisa raised her voice and said, "Ah, Mom, give me a break! Everyone is online right now! I'll be off soon."

Explain the path you then took, using any positions and techniques used. Write in the form of a list if it's easier.

1. *I said, "No! I said no!" (Back-to-back)*

2. *Lisa rolled her eyes.*

3. *I unhooked from the situation, literally left the room for about two minutes. Lisa stayed on computer. After thinking about it (took a look), realized another few minutes would actually not be such a big deal. She'd worked hard that evening to complete a tough math assignment.*

4. *Went face-to-face and told Lisa another few minutes would be OK. I told her I knew she'd worked hard all evening and therefore she could stay on the computer until 9:45 p.m.*

5. *Lisa was appreciative and apologized for her outburst.*

6. *At 9:45 she got off Facebook and turned off her computer.*

Technique(s) used: Unhook and take a look; was successful

Resolution: Not really, still need to discuss the general issue of time on the computer and how it seems to be eating into home-work time. Will suggest five more minutes two times a week as long as Lisa continues to respect the boundaries I set—and that includes no Facebook or IMing.

Now that we've discussed the different steps of the Chair Strategy, I hope you will begin to use them in your interactions with your daughter. Let them work for you and see what a difference they can make in your relationship:

Step One: Observing and identifying chair positions

Step Two: Changing chair positions to work through conflict

Step Three: Navigating through positions to arrive at a resolution

In the final part of the book we will look at how mothers just like you have used the Chair Strategy to help them tackle some of par-enting's thorniest subjects: sex, money and values, and divorce.

Nina at LAX

Nina was a sixty-three-year-old career waitress whom I met at the Los Angeles International airport when we were both in line at the gift shop. She was holding a bundle of magazines and snacks. When a few items fell out of her arms and onto the floor, I offered my assistance. As I handed back the final item, I couldn't help but notice a real sadness in her eyes when she thanked me.

"You OK?" I asked.

"Ehhh," she groaned.

It doesn't take a psychiatrist to know that when you get a response like that, particularly from a stranger, it's an open invitation to pry. So I did.

"Lot of stuff you're buying there," I remarked. "Long flight?"

"Oh, you have no idea," she replied.

Clearly, this woman was desperate for someone to talk to. So after Nina and I paid for our items, we walked into the airport terminal and sat down together. Within about five minutes, I knew the broad strokes of her life story as well as the reason for the sadness in her eyes.

Nina and her twenty-five-year-old daughter, Joan, hadn't spoken in two years. Communication abruptly ended between them when Joan eloped with a man Nina and her husband felt was bad news. He had no job, no visible means of support, and he convinced Joan to move to Ohio with him to start a new life together. Though Nina didn't think the young man was dangerous, she got a bad vibe from him. She begged Joan to stay away from him. Young and in love, Joan defied her parents and moved with the man to Ohio.

For six months, Nina reached out to Joan with calls and e-mails. Joan never responded to any of them. With no financial resources to travel, Nina could do nothing but accept what she knew was the biggest heartache of her life, losing her daughter. Completely devastated, Nina went into a depression and was never the same.

The week I met Nina, she had gotten a call from an old high school friend of Joan's. The friend told Nina that Joan was quite ill with breast cancer and told her where she was living. At that point, Nina's friends and neighbors pitched in for a plane ticket. Nina was on her way to see Joan that day.

"That is an amazing story," I said. "*You* are amazing."

She turned bright red. "I'm not amazing, I'm horrible." She began to cry. "I'm a horrible person and a horrible mother. I am ashamed of myself."

It was difficult at this point to offer any real comfort to Nina, as she was virtually a stranger. At the same time, I felt a connection to her and her story.

"Nina," I said, "what you are doing is a brave and loving thing. And the circumstances that brought you to this point don't really matter right now. What's important is that you are going to see Joan and will be there for your daughter."

She thanked me, offered me a pack of gum, and then realized it was just about time to board her plane.

"Do me one favor," I said. "Write down these four things for when you and Joan have a chance to talk."

"Oh, God, is this some kind of weird psychic thing?" Nina asked.

"Actually, no," I said. "It's some kind of weird psychiatrist thing."

"I'm afraid of shrinks," Nina said.

"Me too."

We both laughed. She took out a piece of paper and, per my request, wrote down the following:

1. Connect your head to your heart.
2. This is your opportunity.
3. Open your mind to what she says.
4. Be aware of yourself.

She folded up the paper, put it in her purse, and left to board the plane.

The Chair Strategy:
Frequently Asked Questions

Will this really work for my daughter and me even if our current relationship is stormy?

Stormy may very well be the reason you bought this book. Yes, it will really work. Furthermore, it would be highly unusual if your relationship wasn't stormy at times. But remember that it may have taken years for the two of you to get to the place where a back-to-back position is your natural stance. If that is the case, it will take time to redirect your position. But with consistency and an unwavering commitment to improvement, you will see positive changes.

Is it too late to have a better relationship if my daughter is grown up with kids of her own?

It is never too late. But remember, it will take time. I've seen countless relationships transformed using these techniques. There's no reason why it can't work for you and your daughter too. (And why not buy your daughter her own copy of this book?) Importantly, not only will the techniques you apply from this book help your relationship with your daughter; they will help your daughter's relationship with your granddaughter. Remember, much of our own behavior is modeled on our parents'.

What if one of us gets really upset, cries, and wants to stop talking?

That's perfectly OK and is to be expected at some points. If you communicate your need to unhook respectfully, the other should comply and resume when you are ready. One of you cannot force her will on the other, and progress will continue when both of you are ready.

Is the Chair Strategy something we should practice even if we are getting along?

Yes. The Chair Strategy is a way of viewing communication with your daughter at all times. As you incorporate it into your life, it will become second nature and the only way you and your daughter communicate. Indeed, you will be unaware you're doing it.

Sometimes I just want to yell at my daughter. What if I get tired of this style of communicating?

When you yell (or want to), make note that you're likely in a back-to-back posture and then work to move out of it. Bear in mind, though, that the intention of the Chair Strategy is not to make mother-daughter communications robotic. Of course there will be times of heightened emotions. Throughout this book I've emphasized the obvious fact that both you and your daughter are human beings. You are learning an entirely new way of communicating, so don't hold yourself to unrealistic standards. Some people may even feel disconnected when they are no longer relating in the back-to-back position (see box on page 137 on back-to-back junkies).

What if my daughter won't work with me using this strategy?

As noted above, you cannot force your will on her, but I always remind people that change begins with you. Try these techniques with your daughter and see what happens. If she doesn't get the usual reaction from you, she will have no other option but to try another way to communicate effectively. And she will begin to mimic your efforts.

Should I tell others in my life that I am trying this strategy?

Hopefully these people will begin to see and hear the changes as they unfold, due to the improved relationship you'll have with your daughter. That said, sharing the Chair Strategy is a wonderful idea. The Chair Strategy is not designed to separate the world into an enlightened group of haves and the doomed-in-relationship-hell have-nots. But you have made a personal commitment to improving your relationship with your daughter, and this book provides concrete tools and real-world examples to help you achieve your goal.

What if I need more information or have a question for you, Dr. Sophy?

I can always be contacted through www.drsophy.com to answer any questions you may have. Also, check my Web site periodically to see my blogs on various topics.

PART THREE

Hot-Button
Issues

Your daughter is human. I state the obvious to remind you that even with your love, strength, and conscientious role-modeling to guide her, she will make choices throughout her life that will upset, disappoint, or anger you. This is to be expected. The opposite is also true. Your daughter will act in ways that will surprise—even thrill you. Regardless, it is your daughter's experiences that matter, not yours. Your job is to guide her with honesty and clear, age-appropriate communication, which the Chair Strategy has equipped you to do quite effectively at this point.

Nonetheless, there are certain topics that have the potential to sidetrack even the most seasoned of parents: sex, money and values, and divorce. The emotions these issues incite may complicate the mother-daughter dynamic in unexpected ways, making you feel as if all of the unconditional love and respect you've given your daughter has not made a bit of difference. This is not true. When one of these loaded issues arises, she needs your attention, love, and guidance more than ever.

In the following chapters, you will be able to take a close-up look at real mothers and daughters as they tackle these hot-button issues using the Chair Strategy and its basic techniques. One of the points you will observe is that there is no magic formula. The magic—in this case, landing side-by-side—happens only with real commitment, honesty, and trust in the process, something that you have shown since we began our journey. Though I use the same techniques, assessments, and exercises for everyone, these cases employ slight variations of the step-by-step process laid out in part two. This is because, as the third-party navigator and expert, my job is to look at each situation and take into account such variables as the mom and daughter's immediate needs, the time frame, and any other particulars that inform my plan of action. The more you embrace the Chair Strategy, the more you will see your own individualized approach start to emerge. Along with that, you and your daughter will more easily achieve a side-by-side resting place on the difficult issues that come your way.

CHAPTER

8

Sex and the
Perceived Transfer
of Sexuality

A FIFTEEN-YEAR-OLD PATIENT OF MINE, Alicia, was having a difficult time socially. Though she had plenty of friends at school, both male and female, the problem for her was that her girlfriends were starting to date but none of the boys seemed interested in her. Alicia was a straight-A student, outgoing, and well liked by her peers. If I were to describe her physical appearance individually—long, wispy blond hair, large blue eyes, and porcelain skin—you might imagine a beautiful young woman. However, for Alicia, these attributes yielded quite a plain Jane. Her transition to young womanhood, particularly in the eyes of the boys, was not happening. She believed her status as the funny one among her guy friends kept her in the friend zone. It bothered her greatly and had started to affect her schoolwork.

In our first session together, after talking about her S.W.E.E.P., Alicia mentioned that she had never had a real conversation with a grown-up about sex. The only information she got was as a

161

seven-year-old when she had asked her mom how a woman got a baby in her stomach. Mom told Alicia that babies started to grow when two people who loved each other very much hugged tightly. That was the entire conversation.

Alicia told me that soon after this talk, her Uncle Joseph came into town for a visit. She adored her uncle and was very excited to see him. When he arrived at their house, Uncle Joseph greeted her as he always did—with open arms. She remembers how scared she was when he picked her up to give her a great big hug. As she struggled to escape his grasp, she said, "Please put me down! You're hugging me too tight."

Alarmed, Uncle Joseph replied, "Sorry, honey, I didn't realize . . ."

With that, he placed Alicia back down.

Alicia responded, "Thanks. I just really don't want to have a baby."

At that point, Alicia remembers her mom giggling and saying, "That's so funny!" Alicia was confused and embarrassed but said nothing—and neither did her mom. Although on some level Alicia knew that babies probably didn't come into the world that way, she continued to avoid tight hugs.

Nothing could be more dangerous in leading your daughter down her emotional path than offering her a back-to-back stance on the issue of sex. Sexuality is one of the key components that define who your daughter is. Although she must explore this area for herself and in her own time frame, it is a mom's responsibility to keep a respectful eye on her child and help guide her through this very personal process. This duty begins sooner than most moms realize.

It is astonishing to me the number of moms who believe the best way to handle this issue is to keep their daughters in the dark—and away from the opposite sex—for as long as possible, rather than to educate them. This attitude almost always stems from the mother's anger and resentment over her own unhappy experiences with the opposite sex. Not only is this harmful to a daughter, but it is completely unfair. Though it should go without saying that when it comes to sex, physical protection is crucial for your daughter (for example, by using a condom), there is no reason and nothing to be gained from emotionally or intellectually shielding her from sex and sexuality. Ever.

I understand that talking to your daughter about sex can seem daunting. It doesn't have to be. And that should never be a reason to avoid the topic altogether. When should you begin to address the idea of sex or sexuality with your daughter? Some moms believe this is accomplished with the proverbial birds-and-the-bees chat that often occurs after your three- to five-year-old asks, "Where do babies come from?" Though every parent conducts this talk with her own sense of style and according to her child's developmental stage, it is one of those parental responsibilities that is almost always anticipated with dread. Typically, the goal is to get it over with to minimize the parent's discomfort. As we saw with Alicia, this gets in the way of what should be one of the real goals: helping your daughter make sense of things. Though the brief and vague explanation about the mechanics of reproduction may satisfy your daughter for the moment, it can't begin to equip her in any effective way for what is ahead. Another goal is to open up the lines of communication so that as your daughter matures she will feel comfortable coming to you with her questions and concerns.

Your words are powerful, mom. The way you talk to your daughter about sex can enlighten her or, as was the unfortunate case for Alicia, confuse her. Here she was, on the cusp of womanhood, and she was clueless about her blossoming sexuality. No doubt her social ineptitude had been shaped in part by her mother's back-to-back stance on the topic of sex. Whereas I am endorsing that education and knowledge be transferred from mother to daughter about sex and sexuality, I am not suggesting that you promote sex to your daughter. Discussing abstinence is always an option as long as you are clear to your daughter exactly from what it is she should be abstaining.

The Dos and the Don'ts:
Talking to Your Daughter about Sex

Ages 3–7

Do take your daughter's lead. If she is asking questions about private body parts or is curious about where babies come from, she is sending you a message that she wants some information. Greet her face-to-face and hear what she has to say and wants to know. Let her do the talking at first. It is your job to listen and respond with age-appropriate, honest answers.

Don't avoid the topic because you are uncomfortable. This will send an unintended message to your daughter that sex is not something we talk about or that sex is an uncomfortable topic. Wrong. Sex is something we must talk about. The moment you greet her back-to-back on this topic, you set an unhealthy precedent.

Ages 7–12

Do expect questions with more detail and that involve a real person, such as, "Cousin Jenna is pregnant. How does that happen?"

Don't expect immediate understanding. Remember, these are difficult concepts to grasp. Give her time, space, and an opportunity to talk.

Do expect her information to be varied. At this point, she has heard bits and pieces from several sources—friends, the media, and so on.

Don't react with emotion to any of the things she may ask.*

---

*If you do find yourself getting emotional, go back to your journal entry about unmet needs and see if you can figure out what may be causing these reactions.

By age twelve or thirteen, your daughter should have a clear picture of sex and reproduction. Even before your daughter speaks, she has learned about sex and sexuality from you. She is absorbing:

- The way you dress

- How you demonstrate affection toward your husband or partner

- Your interactions with men in general

- What she sees on TV and in the media

- What she hears at school and from peers

All of this makes mothering a daughter quite complicated. But in my opinion, there is one potential complication in this arena that trumps all others: Perceived Transfer of Sexuality (PTS). I coined this phrase to describe a phenomenon that is prevalent among my patients, regardless of their background or socioeconomic status. PTS is a feeling that many moms have that their daughters are somehow taking away their own sexuality or trumping it. The key word here is *perceived*. Remember, perception is powerful. And in PTS, perception can lead to a subconscious and dangerous feeling of competition between a mother and her daughter. In fact, PTS is responsible for some of the most volatile interactions I have ever witnessed.

PTS doesn't happen overnight. It takes years for these seeds of discord to grow into this type of intense back-to-back positioning. Typically, PTS occurs as a daughter crosses that threshold from childhood to young womanhood. That is the time when something snaps in mom. Up to this point she has been the role model for her daughter and a reflection of what the daughter has aspired to be. PTS turns that mirror around; now daughter becomes a haunting reflection for mom, a reminder of what once was or what will never be.

In some ways, PTS can be seen as an extreme version of the Four Truths converging at once:

1. Both mother and daughter want the same things: love, understanding, respect—and in this case, to be seen as a woman of value and worth. According to the standards of society, this would include an assessment of her sexuality: is she attractive, desirable, and so on.

2. Both mother and daughter speak the same language. That mutual language can be used as a weapon in this most delicate of issues. When it comes to sexuality and the emotions it stirs up, it's no surprise that the conversations between mom and daughter can be volatile.

3. On some level, mother and daughter are in competition with each other. Earlier we discussed several ways in which this competition can play out; when its goal is the acquisition of love and intimacy (even if it's only *perceived*), the communication challenge can be particularly heated.

4. Both mother and daughter have estrogen. Again, within a struggle or competition (or a perceived competition), this hormone can make someone who is on your side seem like an enemy or cause an innocent mistake to be viewed as malicious intent. In PTS, estrogen fuels the fire and a slip of the tongue can become WWIII.

As previously discussed, these Four Truths laid the groundwork for the storm in terms of your relationship with your daughter. It should help to emphasize that this situation is not uniquely yours.

Understanding PTS

There are two basic reasons for PTS:

1. If a woman, prior to becoming a mother, has been showered with attention for her beauty, professional success, or other accomplishments, the perception that her daughter has taken that from her will be experienced as a profound

loss to her sense of self. Mom may perceive this loss as being due to her age, normal body changes, menopause, or her daughter coming of age. This typically causes mom to direct her resentment and anger at her daughter, both consciously and subconsciously. If mom has not done her up-front work, this can be disastrous for her psyche and of course for the relationship she has with her daughter. This kind of reaction is about the mother's needs (for love, attention, validation, and self-worth) no longer being met. Mom must figure out why these needs are no longer being fulfilled. For starters, mom should be paying close attention to what her S.W.E.E.P. checklist looks like and seek to address any imbalance.

2. If in earlier days mom never received the attention she desired—whether it was for beauty, talent, academic achievement, or an unusual ability of some kind—her daughter is then used to obtain this goal so that mom will finally get the prize she never got. This, of course, is all about unfulfilled needs. However, mom can be jealous that her daughter is winning a game that mom never got to play. Sometimes, mom can be resentful that the daughter is being a traitor by playing into society's view of women (as being valued only for her physical attributes, for example), a mind-set that the mother has fought to reject.

This perceived transfer of sexuality could be based in reality. If a mom who was once a celebrity now has a famous daughter, for example, it may seem to mom that her sexuality or fame has been transferred to or even stolen by her child. Realistically, of course, that can't happen. If a beautiful woman is alone in a room and another beautiful woman walks in, the first woman doesn't suddenly lose her looks or become less sexually attractive. But perceived transfer of sexuality is not about reality. It's about *perception*. In mom's view, if she was once considered a great beauty but those days are long gone and now her daughter is getting that kind of attention, it may very well feel as if her own daughter has taken away her attractiveness, and thus her power.

Perceived transfer can literally begin as early as when a daughter is born, and a mother's feelings of inadequacy can linger until the moment she dies. If left unexamined, PTS can cause an irreparable rift in a family and in the bond between mother and daughter.

For better or worse, despite decades of the women's movement and the countless females who hold visible and esteemed positions in government, media, law, academia, and business, women are viewed by our society as sexual objects. The message embedded in our culture is that women need to be pretty and, by extension, a woman's value to society is fundamentally wrapped up in her attractiveness, her ability to find a man to marry, and ultimately, her ability to have children. Of course, some of this is biological; it's imperative we reproduce for the continuation of the species.

Yet there is an even more insidious element at work here regarding cultural standards. What does the ideal woman look like? If you go by what the media tells us, she's a very thin young woman who is sexually promiscuous, with flawless skin, unnaturally white teeth, and voluptuous breasts. In addition, in some quarters a woman's value is still based upon the kind of man she can attract and marry, rather than on her own accomplishments. Is it any wonder so many women live in fear of losing their looks? It is such a vital part of their identity. Finally, as American women age, they tend to feel marginalized by society, finding it harder to be seen as a sexual being even though in some form the sex drive remains with us until we take our last breath.

Perceived transfer of sexuality can be implicated in a woman's jealousy that her husband seems to be paying more attention to his daughter than to her. It can be seen as the reason why some mothers try to blur the boundaries between their daughters' friends and their own; it can even be the reason why a mother makes an overture to her daughter's boyfriend (here's to you, Mrs. Robinson). The perceived transfer of sexuality is often subconscious and therefore hard to identify—not to mention difficult for the mom to acknowledge. A woman has to be brutally honest about her life in order to see the signs of this poisonous perception.

Now that you understand how this phenomenon works, let's look at a couple examples of how it plays out in the lives of actual mothers and daughters.

Stephanie and Liza

Stephanie, a forty-one-year-old divorced mom, called to make an appointment for her and her nineteen-year-old daughter, Liza. Based on the fact that they were both adults, I thought it was appropriate for both of them to attend the initial meeting. This would allow me to observe their interactions and then determine the next steps. All I knew from the initial call was their ages and that the issue was about sex.

The day of the appointment, mother and daughter arrived separately. Though they lived together and were both coming from home, the two of them weren't speaking and couldn't bear to share even a car ride to my office. The two of them were in a searing back-to-back position.

Stephanie arrived first. If there had been any kind of spark in her eye, the outfit and hairstyle she came in with (both a decade out of date) may have gone unnoticed. Instead, she was glaringly unfashionable with a sadness and exhaustion about her. Without wasting a moment, she headed to a chair and plopped herself down, as if the action alone would bring her some relief. Several minutes later, Liza strode in, full of energy and confidence. Her casual bohemian attire reflected this as well. Though she was petite in stature, everything else about her seemed big—her personality, her opinions, her passion. She was nobody's fool. Liza noticed her mom sitting there and, without missing a beat, grabbed the empty chair next to her and slid it as far away from her as my office space would allow. Thankfully that was only about five feet!

There was complete silence in the room. A few minutes later, I spoke up.

Dr. Sophy: So, are you two not speaking?

They both shook their heads.

Dr. Sophy: How did you share information about this appointment?

Liza: Texted.

When a mother-daughter pair comes to see me while in a back-to-back position—particularly when they're not speaking—I begin by giving them a general sense of the Chair Strategy. I did this with them and quickly established the Rules of Talking.

Dr. Sophy: So you see how the two of you are in a back-to-back position?

Both nodded.

Dr. Sophy: Liza, did you notice how you literally came in and moved your chair away from your mom?

She nodded, and smirked.

Dr. Sophy: So our first goal here today is for the two of you to actually speak to each other and move into a face-to-face position to work through your conflict. Understand?

Both nodded, this time in full agreement. I held up my well-worn Rules of Talking sign:

The Rules of Talking

1. Respect each other by listening.
2. Do not speak when the other is speaking.
3. Let the other person finish, even if you disagree.
4. Choose an established signal that lets the other person know you would like to talk.

Stephanie suggested a hand wave as their signal; Liza nodded in agreement. After another long, silent pause:

> Dr. Sophy: Who wants to begin?

> Liza: Me.

Mom nodded.

> Dr. Sophy: Go ahead, please.

> Liza: OK, so basically the problem here, Dr. Sophy, is that this lady (pointing to her mom) treats me like I'm a child and I'm sick of it. (Pause) Oh, and I think this will be a huge waste of my time.

Though still heated, they were now in a face-to-face position. Liza looked over at her mom, who was teary-eyed at this point. Stephanie waved her hand.

> Stephanie: You are only nineteen years old and still living at home. I am the mother here, you are my child, and you are too young to be having sex!

> Liza: No, I'm not a child, I'm an adult! Hello, I'm nineteen. I'm going to college and yes, I'm having sex. And guess what, Mom. I love it!

Mom cringed.

> Liza: Why can't you support that?

> Stephanie: Are you kidding? How can I support that? You're only nineteen, and (turning to me) she's having sex on first dates! It's dangerous! Tell her, Dr. Sophy. Tell her why that's dangerous. She doesn't believe me.

> Liza: This is crazy. Why am I here?

> Dr. Sophy: First of all, let's reestablish the Rules of Talking.

I held up the sign again.

Dr. Sophy: Now, in response to your previous request for me to tell your daughter about safety, I assume the two of you have had this conversation already. This is not my job today. However, I can help you two with the real work that needs to be done so you can better communicate on this subject and in general.

Liza: Mom, listen to me. I had sex on a first date only one time, one time. And I practice safe sex, you know that.

It was clear to me that mom did know Liza practiced safe sex (whether or not mom was responsible for providing that lesson) and was merely using it as a way to reach out to me in an attempt to gain an ally.

Mom turned to me.

Stephanie: She left a condom in my guest room toilet! Nice, huh, Dr. Sophy?

Liza: Oh, OK, guess you'd rather I didn't use one?

Liza turned to me.

Liza: Nice, huh, Dr. Sophy?

Stephanie: That's enough! Stop it, Liza!

Liza: No, you stop it, Mother! Maybe if you had sex every once in a while, you wouldn't be so damn uptight!

Emotions flared and the disrespect brought them again into a back-to-back position.

Then there was silence.

Dr. Sophy: Stop, please, look at your chairs. Do you see how you have moved into a back-to-back stance?

There was about a minute of quiet between them. Mom began to cry hard.

Liza: OK, Mom, I agree that you didn't need to see the condom. I'm sorry about that. But I refuse to apologize, much less feel guilty, for having sex.

Mom was a total mess, distraught over her daughter's actions. And Liza felt good about hers. She had, in fact, taken proper precautions, both with a condom and birth control (I later found out), acting responsibly on behalf of herself and her body. (Leaving behind the condom was another issue, and at this point I was unsure if it was purely unintentional.)

I requested to have thirty minutes alone with each of them, starting with mom. During that time, the other one stayed in the waiting room.

Stephanie

I learned a lot of important information about Stephanie in our time together. She had married her high school sweetheart when she was nineteen years old (interestingly, the current age of Liza), and divorced him ten years later. During the marriage, they had two children together. Liza, the first child, was seven at the time of their breakup and her sister, Renee, was three. Stephanie and her ex-husband shared custody of the children, but mom was the primary caretaker. Since the divorce, Stephanie had not gone out on a single date, claiming, "No time, no interest." In the last several months, though, one of her closest friends had renewed her efforts to get her out of the house, to join a group of some kind, maybe even an online dating service, so that when she had more time in the fall (when Liza would be living on campus), she'd have more of a social life. Stephanie was considering doing this. One of the reasons why Stephanie was prompted to seek help with Liza was so she could raise Renee "better" or at least differently.

As usual, we went over her S.W.E.E.P.:

Sleep: Stephanie hadn't had a good night of sleep in over three weeks, as she was particularly upset over this current impasse with her daughter. In general, she didn't love anything about her bedroom—the sheets were old, the desk cluttered. She spent as little time in the room as possible.

Work: She had worked at the same company for fifteen years and for the most part felt comfortable and happy there. She felt certain the job was hers for life, and therefore she would never have to rely on a man for financial security. Although she didn't earn as much as she felt she should, there were real benefits to the job, such as a generous retirement plan.

Eating: She and Liza rarely shared a meal together. Liza was a college student who hung out on campus with her friends until early in the evening. Because Renee was involved in a variety of after-school activities, the two of them only had dinner together on occasion. Stephanie had put on about ten pounds in the last six months. She was experiencing a premature perimenopause.

Emotional Expression of Self: Stephanie certainly had no sexual intimacy, but she had close women friends with whom she felt a deep emotional connection.

Play: She made very little time for fun. She was all about work. She used to sew quite a bit and enjoyed creating outfits for her girls, but had given it up. Exercise was not part of her life.

Based on this brief time with Stephanie, it was clear that she was going through a perceived transfer of sexuality with her daughter. Stephanie's regrets and unmet needs resulting from her limited sexual journey were getting in the way of her relationship with Liza. As is often the case, PTS reared its head at a time when Liza desperately needed her mother's insights and guidance as she was becoming a sexually active young woman. Stephanie was incapable of offering this to her, of course, as she was crippled by her own "stuff."

Dr. Sophy: Are you jealous of Liza?

She took a moment. Her eyes teared up in what we both recognized as acknowledgment.

Stephanie: Yes.

This was the moment when Stephanie began to get in touch with her perceived loss. On some level, she was resentful of Liza and viewed her as the reason why her life had become so empty. Once she began to recognize the subconscious competition going on between her and her daughter, she was able to address it with honesty. In this way, Liza could be viewed as an opportunity, a shift mom needed to make.

In Stephanie's case, acknowledging jealousy toward Liza was the first step. As an adult female, Stephanie had occasionally experienced jealousy or even healthy competition, but only with women in her peer group. The biggest *aha* moment came toward the end of our time together when Stephanie realized that Liza's age (nineteen, the same age when Stephanie had married Liza's dad) was a source of pain not simply because her baby was growing up but because it underscored how young and naïve *she* had been when she'd made such a serious commitment. (In later sessions, we dealt with this more fully.)

Stephanie never had much of a chance to experience life as an independent woman, much less a sexually free one. Because she went from dating her high school sweetheart to marrying him, her own daughter's life on several levels now troubled her. Subconsciously she was angry and resentful of her daughter's opportunity to enjoy and experience life in a way that had eluded her. What made it worse for Stephanie was the thought that it might be too late for her to have intimacy and romance in her own life. Maybe she was too old. In her view, it was her daughter's time now, and her time was over. I asked Stephanie to begin taking a look at this, and gently suggested that it was important that she get her needs in check. Stephanie had more than enough time—she was only forty-one, after all—to begin anew and date again.

The first point Stephanie and I addressed in terms of Liza was whether or not there was a legitimate reason for mom to be concerned about her daughter's sexual activity. At this point, my guess was that this was not a real issue, as Liza seemed quite responsible about her approach to having sex.

In the meantime, I met with Liza.

Liza

The first exercise I did with Liza, as always, was talk about her S.W.E.E.P. Here's what I learned:

Sleep: Liza slept pretty well, although college was stressing her out a bit. Like her mom, she didn't love her bed or her sheets. Apparently the beds and bedding hadn't been updated in quite a while. Sleep was never an activity viewed as a sacred time.

Work: As a college freshman, Liza was all about school. She cared about her grades and worked really hard. She had nice friends with whom she studied. Her grades were good, and she was very focused on her goal of becoming a journalist.

Eating: Liza had healthy eating habits, and she stayed on campus just about every night to eat with friends.

Emotional Expression of Self: Though not in a steady relationship, she was sexually active. I was struck by how freely she expressed her opinions, including about her parents' breakup, her mother's shortcomings as a parent, and her father's attempts to remain actively involved in her and her sister's lives—despite some interference from Stephanie.

Play: She and her friends loved to work out together and go to the movies. Liza also enjoyed running and all sorts of outdoor activities. This helped her to stay focused on school and to blow off steam as needed.

Overall, Liza seemed to be a well-adjusted, confident, and directed young woman. She was really happy in life, but admitted to feeling sad for her mom. She felt her mom was lonely and had spent the last decade "doing nothing" with herself. As we talked, Liza said that she didn't know what she could do to help her mother.

> *Liza: I know Mom loves me, but she's way too overprotective, and it's getting hard to deal with.*

At that point, I asked Stephanie to join us so we could end this first session together. I wanted these two to leave my office in a face-to-face position and to be able to maintain that stance until the next time I saw them, which would be in two weeks. In the meantime, their assignments were:

- To communicate only using the rules established in our session together—and to respectfully stop talking if these rules could not be followed.

- To have a face-to-face discussion about sex. I wanted them to both keep an open mind as together they explored vital information about sexual activity, AIDS and other sexually transmitted diseases, and birth control. Mom's additional task was to view Liza not simply as a daughter she loved but as a woman in her own right.

- To have a face-to-face discussion on the nature of intimate relationships with the opposite sex, specifically, the emotional component. Liza had never witnessed a loving relationship between her parents, and she had never seen her mom go on a date after her divorce. Even though Stephanie's experiences in this area were quite limited, mother and daughter still needed to connect on these issues.

- To let the other person know that they each trusted the other's judgment and were respectful of each other's decisions, regardless if they agreed with them.

- To have dinner together at least once a week. Renee could come, too.

- To show their affection for each other in some way before leaving my office.

Once they were clear about their homework, the two of them hugged (clearly a positive sign) and walked out of my office.

Two Weeks Later

Liza and Stephanie had driven together to my office. After greeting me, they each grabbed a chair—which I had purposefully moved far apart to see if they would reposition the furniture—and pulled them closer together. I was so glad to see that. Then they filled me in on their activities of the past two weeks:

- They had gone out to dinner and a movie—just the two of them—the first week. During that time, they had a good talk about the emotional aspects of sex and sexual relationships in general. For most of her adult life, Stephanie believed that being in love was a prerequisite for having sex (or that it should be). Although she was trying to broaden her perspective, this continued to be the attitude she hoped Liza would adopt.

Stephanie also spoke about how, in the early years of her marriage, the combined emotional and physical safety of a monogamous relationship had allowed her to experience greater intimacy with her spouse. Though previously Stephanie had felt her reactions to Liza's behavior stemmed from a desire to protect her, she was starting to realize—albeit painfully—that her response was due in part to her subconscious jealousy. In truth, Stephanie had been trying to deprive Liza of experiences that she thought were no longer available to her.

- The second week they had taken an early-morning hike, during which they talked in detail about the physical aspects of sex, including the risks of STDs. Stephanie spoke about the physical safety factor in having a limited number of partners as well as the importance of being able to trust your partner—not only when it comes to sex but in other ways, too.

- They made a pact that once a week the two of them would do an activity together—a hike, a bike ride—while they continued their discussions.

- Liza had sex one time during those two weeks (and practiced safe sex). For the first time, they were able to discuss sex openly because of their work together. Stephanie began to understand Liza's attitude about sexual freedom. This made Liza feel closer to her mom because finally she felt her mom respected her not just as a daughter but also as a woman. By talking a bit more openly about their intimate experiences, Stephanie went from not wanting to know what her daughter was doing to wanting to be informed as a way to draw closer to her daughter and enrich their connection.

- Stephanie joined a book group.

These were the first signs of what has continued to be an overall strong side-by-side position for these two. Mom had to do all of the up-front work that you have done. Both she and Liza incorporated S.W.E.E.P. into their lives. Additionally, mom worked hard on the First Look exercise of the birth experience as well as the Unmet Needs exercise (as you did in part one). Once she started to incorporate S.W.E.E.P. into her life and to address her needs, she was able to work through her perceived transfer of sexuality. As Liza transitioned toward adulthood, her mom was finally taking care of herself. She was also able to let go and allow her daughter the freedom to take care of her own needs as well. In many ways, they were both growing up and making the transition into adulthood, and they haven't stopped working on their relationship.

Sue and Stella

About a year ago, my answering service let me know that I'd received three calls from the same person in the space of a half hour. I was essentially unreachable at the time, as I was in the emergency room with another patient. The anxious caller refused to leave a phone number until her fourth attempt to reach me. When I was able to return her call, I was greeted by a nearly hysterical voice.

For the third time, mom had caught her twelve-year-old daughter throwing up after dinner. Desperate for guidance, the mom, Sue, asked if I could see her daughter, Stella, as soon as possible. Once I was certain there was no need for crisis intervention, I told mom to come in at four o'clock the following day.

"It's my daughter you need to see, not me!" she insisted. "Don't you understand that?"

I understood completely—much more than I could divulge at this point. After a few moments of convincing, mom agreed to come in the next day. Several hours later, she called my answering service and canceled, citing a scheduling conflict. I contacted her right away, and we rescheduled for the end of the week. An hour before that appointment, she canceled again. That night I called her and explained that if making time to get help for her daughter was truly a priority for her, she needed to commit to a scheduled appointment time. She insisted it was a priority, rescheduled, and again, canceled the night before the appointment.

We had one more round of the cancellation dance. It often continues like this with people who are not quite ready to face the music. If you're wondering why I continue to be so accessible to these people who appear to be disrespecting my time and effort, it's because I know that their resistance is part of what needs to be addressed. They reach out to me in the first place because on some level, they know they need help. What they don't realize is how much help they really need. I was pretty sure this was the case with Sue.

The morning of her 8 a.m. appointment, I sat at my desk and caught up on some reading while I waited for my patient to arrive. At 8:23 a.m., there was still no sign of her and no "I'm running late" call. At 8:25, she walked in . . .

Sue: Sorry I'm late, Dr. Sophy. The line at Starbucks was crazy!

Not exactly the opening line you want to hear from a patient, especially a first-timer and one with such a history of canceling appointments. Sue was very tall and lean. The oversize couture bag strapped across her chest only served to emphasize her thin frame. She was well groomed but wore no makeup, and her thick, dark hair was pulled tight in a ponytail, away from her chiseled face. She had the features of a classic old-world beauty, but my guess was the Botox had left behind too few wrinkles to frame her light blue eyes.

> Dr. Sophy: I'm glad you made it. In the future, though, a call would be appreciated, just so I know you're on your way.

> Sue: OK. I understand.

> Dr. Sophy: Let's have a seat, shall we?

She got situated, removed her bag, and put down her large coffee cup.

> Sue: By the way, I want you to know, I did think about calling you from Starbucks, but couldn't because I left my cell phone in the car and my driver was circling around the block somewhere so I couldn't get it. You get the picture.

Oh, yes, I was starting to get the picture.

She began to fill me in on her daughter. Several weeks ago, she had caught Stella throwing up in the toilet after dinner. Stella insisted she was simply too full from eating.

> Dr. Sophy: And you felt satisfied with that answer?

> Sue: Yes, she had eaten a lot that night and she had to have been really full.

> Dr. Sophy: Is this new, Stella eating a lot?

> Sue: Not really.

> Dr. Sophy: Could it be (gently) that you would have been full if you ate that amount, or do you believe Stella was really full?

> Sue: Stella was definitely full. I know it.

My questions were a way of fishing, and mom did not take the bait—or just couldn't admit to the possibility that there was another explanation for Stella's actions.

We moved on. Mom continued to tell me about that particular week. She had caught Stella throwing up again, and when she questioned her daughter, she got the same response. At that point, mom started to observe her daughter closely and caught her throwing up yet again, days later. This was the third time, and when Sue questioned her daughter, it quickly became ugly.

Dr. Sophy: What did you say to her? Do you remember?

Sue: I told her, "Don't you ever do that again!?" Stella started to cry, agreed to stop, and honestly, I thought we were done with it.

At that point, we went through mom's S.W.E.E.P. Here's what I learned.

Sleep: Mom had no difficulty falling asleep or staying asleep. She said she woke up almost every morning feeling pretty well rested.

Work: Though she had been a fairly successful face model, she stopped working some time ago by her choice. She entertained the idea of one day returning to work in the fashion world, but said for now her child came first.

Eating: Mom enjoyed eating but struggled to maintain her modeling weight. Though she chose mostly healthy foods, she had a sweet tooth, which she occasionally indulged. She enjoyed small meals and preferred to pick at her food.

Emotional Expression of Self: Mom was one of those people who narrated her feelings most of the time. She let you know at every moment whether she was happy, sad, or frustrated with whatever was going on. When I asked about her relationship with her husband, and specifically their sex life, she dodged the question.

Play: Mom took good care of herself. She enjoyed frequent massages, facials, and lunches out with friends. She either played tennis or took a Pilates class on most weekdays, which meant that she was unable to pick up her daughter after school.

Overall, what Sue described was a pretty solid initial S.W.E.E.P., and she seemed to maintain a stable relationship with her husband, family, and friends. However, I could sense that mom was a woman used to getting her way. Her response to my questions about her marriage told me I'd have to continue digging in order to find out what was really going on there. Finally, in terms of remaining active and trying to eat "healthy" in order to maintain her "modeling weight," I wondered if these efforts on her part were to make herself happy, to keep her husband happy, to continue to garner attention from others—or an attempt to maintain control over something in her life since she certainly had no control over her husband or her daughter. I wondered how this would play out in therapy.

Then we talked about Stella's S.W.E.E.P., and though mom liked the idea of looking at these areas for Stella, in her opinion, eating was the only area—albeit a big one—that concerned her. Mom felt Stella was getting plenty of rest, enjoyed school, earned good grades, loved hanging out with her friends, and had many areas of interest. She also told me that Stella had strong ties to her friends and family.

We ended this first session with mom opining that her daughter's throwing up was an isolated problem. It was the only "imperfect" issue in her daughter's life, period.

Sue: So how can we fix that?

I told her that I wanted to see Stella, preferably within the week. She agreed, and we scheduled a meeting for two days later.

Stella walked into my office wearing dark, baggy clothes. Her face had the classic beauty of her mother's, though in truth the preteen was probably five to ten pounds over her ideal body weight, but certainly within the acceptable range for a twelve-year-old girl. Her rosy cheeks, long pigtails, and awkward posture made her appear even younger than she was. There was tentativeness about her. Though it was clear she knew there was a reason she was in a psychiatrist's office, she wasn't exactly sure what would ensue.

After chatting for a few minutes, I asked her about the different areas of her S.W.E.E.P. Her responses created a much different picture than what mom had painted.

Sleep: Most nights Stella had difficulty falling asleep so that, once asleep, she only had a good four to five hours of rest a night.

Work: Although she was keeping up with her schoolwork and her grades were fine, she was starting to feel drained from the emotional and physical energy required to sustain this level of work. She kept at it, though, because everyone else was expecting this of her. She claimed she didn't care about any of this.

At this point, I knew I needed to explore her apathy and determine how pervasive it was. Was she simply bored with school, or was she depressed?

Eating: She told me that sometimes after eating with her family, she felt so full she threw up to relieve herself—yet she did not experience this feeling when she ate with her friends, with whom she liked to eat.

Emotional Expression of Self: Stella was a tad shy and withdrawn when we spoke, but mentioned that she was more talkative with her friends. From her responses, it was clear that she hadn't gotten to the stage where she was interested in expanding her social horizons to include boys.

Play: She had a few close friends but had been withdrawing from them lately. She did not like to exercise at all.

Stella spent most of the session trying to convince me her mom was the one who needed help. It was becoming clearer that it would take some time to get an accurate picture of this situation, so when Sue joined us at the end of our time together, I told the two of them that if they wanted my assistance, seeing them in action on their home turf was key. They both agreed, and I explained that in order for a home visit to show me a real slice of their life, it was crucial for everyone to be themselves and they shouldn't go out of their way to entertain me. I was not to be considered a guest, but rather a piece of furniture with speaking privileges.

I suggested I come for a family dinner, not only because the daughter's symptom involved food but also because the whole dinner experience was a constant in their lives—almost every night this family gathered together for dinner. Stella cited that particular time of day as being very stressful for her ever since she was little.

The Home Visit

I arrived a few minutes before our 6:30 p.m. dinner, leaving just enough time for simple greetings and a quick read of the atmosphere. Mom answered the door, dressed to the nines. No doubt the general population would have assumed she was either still dressed from an event she had attended earlier in the day or had a gala to attend later that evening. As I suspected, neither was true. Rather, as I had requested, mom was true to form, appearing for dinner as she would on any other night—looking as if a camera crew could be popping in at any moment.

Mom clearly loved photo ops. Framed photographs of her were all over the entryway and on the wall next to the staircase. Many of the images were just of her; some also included notable public figures. I saw very few photos of dad or Stella around, and the ones I did see were out-of-date images taken when Stella was a baby. Keeping framed images up-to-date is quite a task, but the lack of photos of the only child in the house seemed significant.

Soon dad came downstairs, dressed in slacks and a shirt. Stella followed, still dressed in her school uniform. Though Stella was sufficiently friendly, dad said very little. Dad's uncomfortable silence spoke volumes. He seemed angry that his daughter was being subjected to this kind of in-home examination, and his

Home Visits

I do home visits for several reasons. Sometimes I visit a home to accommodate a family's busy schedule. Other times, the information gleaned from quietly observing a person in her own surroundings informs my treatment plan. Finally, I may do a home visit to participate in a family activity so that, ideally, I can experience firsthand what I've only heard about in therapy.

Though many professionals (and nonprofessionals) frown upon home visits, considering them controversial or simply taboo, they are a very effective way to gain fresh insights about a family. Traditional mental health professionals see their role in therapy as minimal, and it is the patient who does most of the communicating, both verbally and nonverbally. For the professional, it is about interpreting the verbal. Anything beyond an occasional question or a gentle suggestion from the doctor is considered by many to be crossing a boundary. For those with that mind-set, a home visit is unacceptable. I couldn't disagree more!

Home visits—albeit unorthodox—have brought about successful outcomes for my patients time and time again, particularly for mothers and daughters. Yes, home visits can be extremely intense and explosive, yet at the same time they are completely emotionally and physically safe. The reason: I am right there, guiding the process. It's a perfect way for a family to confront their issues under their own roof, the very place where these issues most likely took root.

actions vacillated between doting on his wife and attending to his daughter. Clearly, he loved them both.

Dinner began. Per usual, it took place in the formal dining room, and everyone sat down in their regular seats: mom at the head, dad to mom's left, and Stella opposite him so they faced each other. When I sat down at the other end of the table, directly across from mom, I noticed the discomfort register on her face.

Their chef served a delicious and healthy dinner. After a few minutes the three of them got caught up in their usual dinner conversation as they each shared bits of their day. I just listened quietly and observed.

Throughout the conversation, mom silently policed Stella's dinner plate, subtly at first. When Stella asked for a second helping of potatoes, mom glared outright at her daughter. Though she didn't say a word, Stella continued to look over at mom in the hope of a sign of approval. She never got one. But then dessert arrived.

The chef brought out a decadent chocolate cake. Stella and her dad each asked for a piece. As expected, size-zero mom passed it up. Stella dug into the dessert as mom tried to contain her mounting disapproval.

Mom: Are you going to eat all of that, honey?

Stella: Yes, why?

Mom: It's just so heavy.

Dad: Yeah, but it's really good.

The anxiety was showing on Stella's face as she took another bite. A big one. With that bite came a sharp, judgmental look from mom. It was clear that mom did not want Stella to eat cake. Without missing a beat, mom picked up her own fork, reached over to Stella's plate, and began to pick at the remnants of her daughter's dessert. This was my perfect (and carefully navigated) opportunity to enter the discussion.

Dr. Sophy: Wow, who doesn't finish chocolate cake?

Stella shrugged and looked down at the table.

Dr. Sophy: I bet you want to, though.

She shrugged again and continued to look down, holding back tears. There was a moment of silence as Stella continued to struggle with what I assumed was a mixture of anxiety, sadness, embarrassment, and anger. Stella typically stuffed these feelings inside—in the form of food—then she regurgitated them later. What I wanted for them, all of them, was to understand what was happening here.

Dr. Sophy: Stella, please tell your parents what you are feeling right now.

Stella: What's the point?

She stood up to leave.

Dr. Sophy: The point is they need to know how you feel.

Stella continued to stare down at the table, and mom looked confused—although I didn't believe she was completely clueless. Mom understood more at this point than she was willing to own. This dynamic seemed quite familiar to everyone at the table.

I explained to Stella how important it was for her to stay at the table and work through this moment. She then looked over at me helplessly. Our eyes met and, without saying a word, she clearly conveyed the message: "This sucks, Dr. Sophy, but OK." Stella let out a big sigh and took her seat again. This small gesture of sitting back down was actually quite huge because here, in her own home and in the midst of the greatest source of her stress, anxiety, and sadness—the family dinner table—she was trusting this process and me. Stella now felt safe. Safe enough to stay. Safe enough to feel. Ultimately, safe enough to communicate with her parents.

It appeared that dad was torn between wanting to comfort both his daughter and his wife. I was hoping that Stella would be the one he'd reach out to. She needed him to do so.

At this point, I turned to mom and dad and asked them what they thought was happening.

> *Dad: I don't know but Stella looks upset.*

> *Mom: I have no idea why she'd be upset right now.*

As mom continued to feign confusion . . .

> *Dr. Sophy: Here's a clue, Mom. You ate her dessert.*

> *Dad: (To mom) Well, that's what you always do.*

> *Mom: No, I don't. That's not true.*

> *Stella: Yes it is, and it makes me really mad.*

A perfect moment in terms of this family's recovery had just occurred. For the first time, daughter had connected her head to her heart and communicated her feelings on this topic. Mom seemed invested in the actions of those around her. Dad finally showed a sign of true connection. At this moment mom and dad both realized that Stella, the one they originally identified as the patient, was merely one of three patients sitting at that dinner table.

That dinner marked the beginning of this family's healing process. In the months that followed, I continued to see Stella and her mother, both separately and together. I also started to see mom and dad once every several weeks. Though Sue had initially sought help because of Stella's food issue, the unfortunate root of this family's trouble was mom's perceived transfer of sexuality to her daughter. So much of Sue's self-esteem was wrapped up with her looks. She still thought of herself as a model, even though she hadn't worked in front of the camera in well over a decade. And here was Stella, a beautiful and capable young woman with her whole life ahead of her. In mom's head it seemed as if Stella was gaining on her. Mom's resentment toward Stella grew, and she became increasingly more threatened by her daughter, whom she felt was somehow becoming (or had the potential to become) the woman she used to be.

A perceived transfer of sexuality can poison even the most solid of mother-daughter relationships. Sadly, though Stella was merely a typical teenager trying to live her life, she was paying a huge price as she rebelled against her mother's control. And dad was caught in the middle.

One of the most significant points Sue began to realize was that, at this point in her life, being a mom was no longer as fulfilling as it had once been. Though she had enjoyed the endless tasks involved in mothering a young child, as Stella got older and needed less hands-on care, Sue was less engaged by this job she had chosen and was searching for other meaningful activities to fill her day. Her husband, actually quite a gentle and loving man, was consumed by his work and didn't really appreciate what his wife was facing. Most of Sue's friends were in a position similar to hers; they often talked in general terms about what they wanted to do with the rest of their lives, but none of them had quite figured it out.

Part of why being a mother had become so unfulfilling for Sue was due to the competition she felt with her daughter. She was so caught up in her own perceived loss, she didn't have the time, energy, or desire to devote to Stella. As a result, their relationship had suffered greatly.

It took a lot of work to get Sue to this point. Here was the overall plan I laid out for her and Stella:

- The initial sessions and home visit began the process by which mom, dad, and daughter came to understand their particular behaviors and family dynamic. For mom, we began her journey through up-front work. And I taught her, along with Stella, the Chair Strategy.

- The first order of business was to deal with Stella's purging. Because it was now out in the open, she wasn't running to the bathroom after dinner as often. Though she would continue her lifelong battle to deal with her emotions in more productive ways (as we all do) as she sorted out her thoughts and feelings, Stella realized the connection between her emotions and food. This element, once under control, made a difference in her schoolwork as well as in her overall relationship with mom. In truth, Stella's purging was collateral damage; the real problem was mom's perceived transfer of sexuality, which was affecting everyone in the family.

- The entire family continued to check their S.W.E.E.P. regularly.

- Our main goal was to transition mom and Stella out of their back-to-back position and toward the more healthy and loving side-by-side stance. They committed to taking weekly mother-daughter walks. In addition, because both mother and daughter liked to write, they found guided journaling to be a very effective means of communication. They began this process by writing about a simple topic in which neither was too emotionally invested yet on which they had different points of view. I suggested they write about a movie they had both seen. This activity served as an icebreaker and allowed them to get comfortable and feel safe in expressing their drastically different opinions in a lighthearted yet passionate way. Essentially, they were experiencing a face-to-face position on the page.

- Next I assigned them a topic that hit closer to home: food. Specifically, family dinnertime. They began by writing about dining out versus home-cooked meals, and then when we were together they would each read their thoughts aloud. Eventually I asked them to dig deeper and explore how food made them feel—if it was relaxing and safe to eat during dinnertime and any potential fears they had about food. Slowly, mother and daughter were working toward their ultimate goal of a side-by-side position as a resting place.

You Are Worthy

As we leave this chapter, I'd like to point out that an important element of PTS is self-worth, which is tied in with self-esteem and self-respect. It is important to have true self-esteem and self-respect in order to feel worthy, valuable, and therefore secure within yourself. When this occurs, you will be able to relinquish what is no longer age-appropriate in your life. In order to retain your sense of self-worth, you must first know who you are and what is important to you; doing your up-front work will help you figure this out. The problem for a lot of moms is that they have been so caught up in attending to the needs of their families that they have neglected to put themselves first. It's a classic scenario. Before mom knows it, the children are older and more independent and don't need her as much . . . and mom is left feeling rudderless. The antidote to this situation, of course, is to consistently do the up-front work so that it becomes a part of your thought process. That way, when you are facing that empty nest, you will be secure in yourself, strong, balanced, and clear about who you are (addressing all of your unmet needs) and ready to start another phase of your life. If you are in this situation, you don't need to do this on your own. Reach out to a supportive spouse, your friends, a trusted member of the clergy, or seek professional guidance or join a support group.

EXERCISE: SELF-WORTH

Turn to a clean page in your journal and write down your responses to the following questions:

> What has my S.W.E.E.P. revealed? Which areas of my life are strong, and which ones need more of my attention?
>
> Am I happy?
>
> Am I confident most of the time?
>
> Do I deserve to feel good, happy, and fulfilled?
>
> Do I spend time giving back to my community?
>
> Are there things in my life that are working against my sense of self-worth?

Now turn to a new page in your journal and fill in the blanks:

> When I do _____, I feel strong and confident.
>
> My most insecure time is when I _____.
>
> My _____ add to my feeling of self-confidence.
>
> If I had more _____ in my life, I would feel better.

All of the above should start you on a process of self-reflection. And remember: People need to define themselves as more than just sexual beings. It is an obvious but painful truth that if your self-worth is tied to your youth, beauty, or sexuality, sooner rather than later you'll feel older, less beautiful, and lacking an identity. Instead of investing all your value in your looks, why not invest in your heart and soul? You have so many dimensions to your life, as a nurturer, or an intellectual, an athlete, a professional—these are all parts of being a woman, and they are all intensely valuable. Life is always about change. As we age it's up to each of us to explore and to grow as people. If we don't, we will stagnate. As your priorities change, it's the perfect time to allow yourself to change along with those priorities. But your sense of worth must remain. No matter what the world thinks of you, what matters most is how you view yourself. Your self-worth is based on growth and insight. Wisdom is something that no one can ever take from you.

CHAPTER 9

Money and Values

A MOM AND HER EIGHT-YEAR-OLD daughter stand in front of a full-length mirror in the Nordstrom shoe department. Together they admire the fancy gold sandals on mom's feet. She rolls up her jeans to get a better view and struts down an imaginary catwalk. Daughter watches with wide-eyed wonder.

Daughter: Mommy, they are so pretty!

Clearly mom agrees as she continues to pose for her daughter. She turns to the salesman.

Mom: How much are these again?

Salesman: The regular price is $175 but they're on sale for $80. They're real show-stoppers.

Mom continues to pose.

Daughter: Please, Mommy, you have to get them!

Mom: I know, I know, they are beautiful . . .

She hesitates, but just for a moment.

Mom: OK, OK, I'll get them . . .

Daughter: Yay!

The two of them do a happy dance over the decision to take the show-stoppers home. Mom takes off the shoes and hands them to the salesman.

Mom: I'll put them on my credit card. (Then turning to her daughter) Hey, sweetie, let's not tell Dad I bought these, OK?

Daughter: Why?

Mom: Well, they're a little expensive, and Dad worries about that kind of stuff. So, it'll be our little secret, promise?

Daughter: Promise.

Not unlike a mother's perspective on sex, her attitude toward money is something she continually conveys to her daughter, both consciously and subconsciously. And the messages her daughter receives are often confusing, as the above scenario makes clear. Here, mother and daughter are sharing an enjoyable experience. And bonding is usually good. However, in this instance, the daughter is being asked to keep this connection private. The justification offered—not to worry dad—may appear loving, but the fact is that mom is asking the child to do something secretive. And the request itself is dishonest. What does that say to her daughter? For starters, it is telling her that if you are secretive, you can get what you want. And in the broader sense, the message is that you don't need to be honest about money . . . and that you don't need to be honest at all if it fits your agenda. If that is mom's intended lesson (and I truly hope that it isn't), then it has most likely been taught. If not, mom needs to understand what her behavior is actually telling her daughter. It is similar to the confusion Alicia experienced regarding her mom's explanation of how babies are made.

Let's play the shoe scenario out a bit. Imagine that the daughter has been yearning for a brand-new Hannah Montana bike. Mom tells her no because it's too expensive. Yet daughter has a good reason to believe that she will indeed get the bike; mom could buy it for her just like she bought herself those shoes. She could say, "We won't tell Dad about the Hannah Montana bike, so he won't worry." Daughter will go home with her new bike just as mom went home with those show-stopping shoes. But in the likely occurrence that daughter doesn't get the overpriced bike, how will mom explain it?

In my practice, I see these kinds of situations all the time. Casual or mixed messages about money can set you up for real conflict with your daughter. It's important to talk the talk and walk the walk. Figure out what you want your daughter to understand about money and tell her with your words *and* actions. In the illustration above, I'm not suggesting that mom deprive herself of the shoes, but that she be honest in her communication with her daughter. If this mom works outside of the home, she could have said: "I am going to buy these shoes. They are expensive, but I work hard and I am making a choice about how to spend our money. If I buy these shoes, then I'll have to cut back in another area." Then mom could talk through the decision-making process with her daughter. In this way, daughter would be taught two important lessons: that in this family we are open and honest with one another, even when we're in a potentially uncomfortable or difficult situation, and that there is a process by which decisions get made. If mom doesn't have a paying job, she could have said, "Daddy works so hard, and these shoes are just not in our budget. Let's call him and see if we can figure it out." Or, "Maybe I won't buy a new dress for the Smiths' party next weekend." This is much more respectful, and shows the value of money and how to prioritize purchases.

On one level, money is a simple concept. Even at an early age, your daughter can learn the basics: that money is a tangible commodity you can hold in your hand or put in a piggy bank to save for a special toy. Along similar lines, she can grasp the concept that money helps us to buy material goods, from basic necessities like food and clothing to luxuries like toys and presents. She watches as you write a check to pay the gas bill or to make a donation to a charity. She is there when you charge a purchase or put an ATM card in a machine and get out cash. Each of these transactions is dependent upon the amount of money you have and your personal preference—how you choose to spend your money.

In our society, money is an even more taboo topic than sex. Overall, it makes most of us uncomfortable. Having a lot of it gives some people permission to act in ways the rest of us consider rude, ugly, immoral—or downright illegal. Not having a lot of it can cause people to act along similar lines too. And when it comes to your daughter, it may be unsettling for reasons you can't quite put your finger on.

One of the reasons why money is such an emotionally charged issue is because it oftentimes is tied in with our feelings about our parents and our own childhood. The complication arises because of this emotional attachment to money and, more importantly, what we buy with it. This is where *value* comes into play. You may value that fancy watch not only because it's a beautiful gift but because of what it represents: status (only people of a certain stature get to wear such an accessory), success (the giver must have a lot of money if he's spending so much of it on a watch), or love (he must really love me if he's willing to spend his money on this object for me).

In my opinion, understanding this distinction is key to how your child views and relates to money. Therefore, your conversations about money should begin with a discussion of values, and not the other way around. Why? Because values are not measured in dollars and cents but instead are based on your personal and unique passions that are informed by all things family—culture, religion, and family history.

It is up to you and your spouse to identify the important values you want to impart to your child: There are no right or wrong answers. Your family may value material goods such as expensive jewelry or luxury cars, or you may treasure experiences with friends, the weekly family movie night, or the monthly shift at the soup kitchen. The amount of money in a family's bank account is no indication of that family's values, particularly the value they place on money itself. Some of the wealthiest people I've treated have some of the most basic and down-to-earth values I've seen—values that place more importance on family dinners than designer handbags. The opposite is also true. Some of the poorest families I work with place a very high value on material goods, will do whatever it takes to acquire them, and regard shared family experiences as less important.

Whatever your family's values are, it is essential that you are mindful of conveying them to your child from the time she is a toddler. Money is just a part of this conversation. Just as it is your responsibility to have the sex talk with your daughter, it is up to you

Assigning Value by Your Reaction

The way a mom reacts to something will send a message to her daughter. That message is part of what helps the child determine how valuable that object is. If a new fur coat makes you squeal in delight, you are placing a high value on that fur coat and your daughter will take in that information. If you express joy in volunteering for your religious institution's annual charity drive, your daughter will get the message that volunteering is a highly prized activity.

You are who you are. Just be aware of how your emotions are shaping your daughter's value system.

to initiate a dialogue about money and values. This task doesn't have to be daunting. However, it's extremely difficult to teach values once the issue of money has been communicated in a back-to-back way. This talk needs to begin in a face-to-face position in order to have a productive exchange of (perhaps opposing) views, and then migrate to a side-by-side dynamic when common ground is found.

Miriam and Tory

When I opened the door to my waiting room, Miriam, a forty-year-old mom and first-time patient, was standing there. She was impeccably dressed—crisp white blouse, black trousers, and coiffed hair—but she possessed, quite honestly, an unfriendly face. It seemed a bit unusual that she was standing rather than sitting and reading a magazine as most of my patients do while they wait. After I introduced myself, she nodded, then marched straight into my office and sat down, not a moment to spare.

Miriam had called me about her ten-year-old daughter, Tory. Her original request was to make an appointment for her daughter, but you know my philosophy . . . and here she was. She launched right into the details about her daughter, a fifth-grader at a local public school. Her behavior in class and at home had recently begun to change quite dramatically. According to mom, Tory, an only child, had always been an "obedient team player" in the family. Over the last several months, though, Tory was becoming more rebellious, refusing to do homework or her chores. Her attitude had become biting and rude toward Miriam.

The final straw for mom was two weeks prior when Tory had stolen gum and candy from their local pharmacy. She had gone with her mom to buy some toiletries and, on the way out, Tory grabbed two packs of bubble gum and a bag of Skittles and quietly put them in her dress pocket. One of the cashiers saw this and alerted the manager. Rather than confront Miriam, a valued customer, the manager left her a phone message. Later, when Miriam called back and heard about this incident, she was angry and confronted Tory immediately, who denied doing it. Finally, though, after threatening her with extra chores, Tory did admit it. At that point, they drove back to the pharmacy and returned the items. Tory was grounded for two weeks and was not allowed to use the phone, computer, or TV. Miriam was so disappointed in Tory, she could barely stand to look her way, and at this point, the tension between them was great.

I asked mom to tell me a little bit about herself. Her one-word response: *organized*. She had always been this way, especially since she'd had Tory. Schedules were her specialty. She had them for everything in her life, from when she slept and ate to doing the grocery shopping and even washing the car. And for Tory as well: bedtime, mealtime, homework, playtime. She told me that the importance of routines and schedules was all she learned from the baby group she attended when Tory was a newborn. At that point, we went through her S.W.E.E.P.

Sleep: "Same time and place," to quote mom. Currently, though, she wasn't falling asleep right away and would toss around for several hours before actually falling asleep. Meanwhile, her husband was snoozing peacefully beside her.

Work: Miriam worked the same type of restaurant management jobs since college. This was never a dream or passion of hers, just a way to "make it and save it."

Eating: The family ate at the same time most nights unless Tory's schedule prevented it. In that circumstance, mom would bring food to wherever Tory was—band practice, a soccer game, and so on.

Emotional Expression of Self: For her, expressing too much emotion was a turnoff, so "I keep mine in check." Miriam's husband was quiet and basically allowed her to run the show.

Play: Miriam exercised daily, usually before bedtime, and she was a voracious reader.

What most concerned me was Miriam's work life, as she was a self-proclaimed workaholic. She explained that she felt strongly about preparing financially for later life, which was something her own parents had failed to do. For many years they had a thriving bakery. Though growing up Miriam always felt financially secure, by the time she got to her senior year in high school, her parents informed her that there was no money for college. When she asked what had happened, her parents had no real explanation other than that they had lived well and planned poorly for the future. Miriam racked up her share of student loans when she went to college.

Several years later, she met her husband. Two years after that, she gave birth to Tory. Her plans were to quit her job and be a stay-at-home mom. Though her husband's job wasn't terribly lucrative, they figured out a way to budget their money for a while until further notice. Their plans changed only a few months after Tory was born. Miriam's parents informed her they were now flat broke and had to sell the bakery. They needed financial assistance desperately, and neither was in good enough health to go out and find other employment. Miriam felt she had no choice but to support them. She resented the fact that she had to leave her baby girl to go back to work to provide for her folks. On the plus side for Miriam, though, was the fact that the apartment she could afford to rent for them was far away and she would now see even less of her parents than before. She paid for their rent, all of their expenses, and gave them a weekly allowance. Seems they too were on one of Miriam's schedules.

As Miriam was telling me this history, she added, "Tory will *never* have to take care of me this way. And she will learn how to take care of herself."

As I continued to listen, it made perfect sense as to why Miriam was a workaholic, and why she didn't want to become a financial and emotional burden to Tory. The problem here was that in her efforts to protect Tory from making the same kind of financial mistakes her own parents had made, Miriam had inadvertently caused another set of problems for her daughter. Whenever I hear a patient talk about not wanting to make the same mistake, it's a signal to me that the person may be making a similar mistake—but by taking the extreme opposite action. In this case, Miriam's inflexibility and micromanaging of her daughter, even with the long-term goal of avoiding this legacy of money problems, was wreaking havoc. In her effort to raise her daughter differently, Miriam, like many moms, was unaware of the negative effects of acting in what she viewed as a more responsible and loving way than her parents did.

As our session came to a close, I shared the basic positions of the Chair Strategy with Miriam and explained how her actions and words were in many ways being delivered in a back-to-back position. Though she was starting to see how her rigidity could very well be described as a back-to-back stance, she did not believe it was the catalyst for some of Tory's behavior. We scheduled an appointment for the following week. I asked Miriam to try very hard with Tory to be face-to-face as much as possible so that they could be in a better place by the time they came to see me, and she agreed.

Two Weeks Later

Tory and her mom arrived for their appointment. Mom marched in as before, with Tory, her obedient foot soldier, in tow. Yet, Tory's mischievous eyes and sarcastic grin let me know that she was contemplating going AWOL. She had a tough look about her and definitely could pass for older, possibly even a young teenager. I asked mom to wait and let us talk alone; she could come in during the final ten minutes of our session. It was up to Tory to reveal exactly what her mother's inflexible handiwork had triggered for her. First, we went through her S.W.E.E.P.

Sleep: Overall her sleep was pretty good. Lately, though, she was more restless than usual.

Work: She had enjoyed school in the past, but this year things had started to change. She was tired of doing homework every night, and she found it difficult to sit through all of her classes. There were just too many rules, and it was starting to feel as restrictive as home.

Eating: She did not like her mom bringing food to her activities. Besides embarrassing her, the food mom brought was way too healthy for her. Lately, she had been sneaking food when mom wasn't around and said her pants were getting tight.

Emotional Expression of Self: Tory was starting to have a few arguments with friends for the first time. She and mom argued constantly because "Mom says *no* to everything." Dad goes along with whatever mom says.

Play: She spent as much time as she could on YouTube, Facebook, texting, and playing soccer.

I asked Tory to be more specific about what her mom would not let her do. Initially, she mentioned the areas where any mom of a ten-year-old would appropriately be setting limits: television watching, computer use, and bedtime. Tory seemed unsettled, though.

> *Dr. Sophy: Is there anything else you'd like to say about your mom saying no?*

She paused for a moment. I could envision the gears turning in her mind as she contemplated exactly how to answer my question.

> *Tory: I don't know. Not really, I guess.*

> *Dr. Sophy: Lots of kids your age get an allowance. Do you receive one?*

With that, the expression on her face changed. It was almost as if a cloud had passed over it.

Tory: Sort of . . . I mean, kind of.

Dr. Sophy: Could you explain what you mean by that?

I knew I had hit a nerve. At this point, she started to cry. As she regained her composure, she revealed that she did receive an allowance, though she was not allowed to spend it. Then she told me she had been saving her money for six months with the understanding that she could buy a Nintendo DS with her savings. When she finally had enough saved, mom refused to let her buy it and instead insisted that all of the money be deposited into Tory's savings account. That was not the plan.

Dr. Sophy: How did that make you feel?

Tory: Mom tricked me. She had been lying the whole time. She never was going to let me buy what I wanted.

Mom's intense and well-intended attempts to protect Tory from the situation she currently was in with her own parents had backfired. It had pushed her daughter to the point of rebellion and even stealing.

Miriam joined us and immediately asked what we had talked about. First we discussed the Nintendo DS and Tory's allowance. For the first time, Tory was able to explain to her mom not just her anger but her disappointment as well.

Tory: I worked very hard to save my money, Mom.

Miriam: Yes, and I work really hard, too, so when you steal gum, I am very disappointed in you. You can't do it! Period!

Tory had approached her mom face-to-face, and Mom responded back-to-back. Tory was shook up and started to cry.

Dr. Sophy: Tory, tell your mom how you feel at this moment.

Tory: I'm disappointed too, Mom.

Miriam: Well, you should be disappointed in yourself!

Dr. Sophy: Is this what you meant, Tory?

Tory shook her head. I asked mom if she had let Tory know what a great job she had done saving, highlighting the strength it took. She hadn't, but was quick to point out again that Tory had stolen the gum by then and allowing her to buy the DS would be rewarding bad behavior. Not surprisingly, mom's instinct seemed to be to start in a back-to-back position. I told mom she needed to acknowledge this strength.

Miriam: OK, Tory. You did a good job saving.

That simple adjustment from mom got a big smile from Tory. And a face-to-face position.

Mom: But I also feel that buying a DS would've been a waste of money and not the kind of thing, Tory, you should be spending money on anyhow.

Dr. Sophy: If Tory hadn't stolen, would you have allowed her buy that DS?

She was silent.

Mom: No, actually. Like I said, it's wasteful.

Dr. Sophy: So in your mind, she would have never gotten to buy the DS, correct?

Mom: Yes.

Dr. Sophy: Would you trust someone who did that to you? Would you trust you?

Tory just stared at her mom, waiting for a response. Miriam was silent for a long pause.

Mom: No, I guess I wouldn't. (Then) I'm sorry, Tory.

Dr. Sophy: Tory, what do you need from your mom in order to trust her again?

Tory: That's easy, Mom. All I want is to be able to spend my money when you tell me I can.

Tory had so looked forward to achieving the goal of saving money to buy something. The fact that it was taken away from her was an extreme letdown—not only because she didn't get the DS, but all of her efforts to save had, in her eyes, essentially been for naught. Finally, mom understood. They had landed side-by-side.

Aside from the fact that mom's rigidity and control was pushing her daughter to rebel, she was sending another message to her: that their family does not value objects of enjoyment, like a Nintendo DS or any typical age-appropriate item her daughter might want. Mom was so afraid that once Tory began to appreciate that you can buy things that bring you happiness or enjoyment, she would want to spend even more money on those kinds of items. In this way, Miriam feared her daughter would turn out like her own mother and never understand how to save, thus repeating the family history. Miriam's tight reins on Tory were working against her to the point of leading Tory to the very place she so desperately didn't want her to end up.

In order for Tory and her mom to get side-by-side, Miriam had to deal with her own issues from childhood (unmet needs) and her interaction with her parents about their lack of financial insight. Eventually, she came to embrace the idea that she had control of the situation with her own family's finances and didn't need to overcompensate in order to prevent a similar outcome. With this freedom came a less rigid, more flexible Miriam.

I asked Miriam and Tory to come back the following week. We spent that entire session on learning the Chair Strategy together and techniques of movement. We also talked about money, values, and the differences between them. Together we came up with a game plan.

- I asked the two of them to use guided journaling to write about the DS incident, as it was significant for both of them. After this, each would read their journal entries aloud and then the two of them were to have a discussion about it.

- Mom committed to finding ways (at least two times a week) to include Tory in financial decisions so that, whether they were shopping for groceries or buying gifts for others, Tory was now a part of the decision-making process. Dad also included Tory in this approach at least two times a week.

- Both had to agree to approach every interaction face-to-face until the next time they saw me. The minute either felt they were in a back-to-back position, she had to stop, unhook and take a look, and pick up again after the heat subsided. In this way, each of them would be able to express their views.

- Both Tory and her mom had to come up with two lists on their own, filled with things they each wanted: "Things I Want That Are Valuable to Me" and "Things I Want That Cost Money." These lists would be updated every two weeks, to keep their money-and-values discussion up-to-date. (See pages 219–220 for exercise.)

One of the positive results of our nation's current economic crisis is the fact that more and more families are finally starting to talk about money. Almost everyone is suffering in some way. I hope you are starting to understand that this is not just because financial cutbacks will affect the food, clothing, and shelter you provide for your daughter. It's because there is the potential for emotional confusion when the basics in your life change—and this goes for adults as well as for children. The next story looks at the fallout from these kinds of changes, although in this instance they are the result of the mom's more deliberate and conscious actions.

Shelly

As I walked down a local street, a woman motioned for me to tell her the time. I stopped for a moment, responded, and then continued on my way. She called after me and asked if I had a few moments to talk about her children. The puzzled look on my face prompted her to tell me that she recognized me from a recent television appearance. Her name was Shelly, and I could see how anxious and jumpy she was. She sat down on a bench, one leg crossed over the other—kicking and twirling her foot as she spoke. She was dressed casually in a T-shirt and jeans, a simple ponytail, and no makeup. I was happy that I did have some time, about fifteen minutes.

I joined her on the bench. She held up the empty bowl in her hand and remarked: "I just ate an entire hot fudge sundae. Oh doctor, if only you had walked by fifteen minutes ago and talked me out of my ice cream pity party!"

We both laughed. Though Shelly's eyes reflected real sadness, she managed to retain a sense of humor. There was an air of confidence about her as well. These were invaluable traits that I knew would serve her well no matter what she was facing. And then she proceeded to tell me her story.

She was a forty-five-year-old mother of three daughters: Allison, age twelve; Lucy, age ten; and four-year-old Rachel. She had been happily married for about sixteen years. She'd met her husband, Seth, at the stationery store she worked at, where she designed invitations. He had come in needing new business cards. They married within the year. At the time, Seth was financially comfortable and ambitiously building a small health-care company. She continued to work and religiously practiced yoga. After their third anniversary, Seth's company went public, and the money began to pour in. Shelly chose to quit her job and, together by conscious choice, the two of them embraced their newfound fortune with abandon. She described the next several years by using the cliché of a champagne-and-caviar lifestyle. "There's simply no other way to put it," she admitted. "It was outrageously indulgent."

Soon after, they decided to build their dream home. Though the luxury vacations and nonstop retail binges continued, Shelly felt the need to do something meaningful. She became extremely involved in a charity, volunteering her time as well as making and raising generous financial contributions. That heartfelt motivation and desire to give back, though, was soon overshadowed by her high-flying lifestyle. She and her husband became the subject of articles in the society pages, and there were various photographs of them in evening attire—Seth in his requisite tuxedo and Shelly in a series of fabulous ball gowns and the extravagant jewelry that accessorized them.

Their first daughter, Allison, was born just as they moved into their eighteen-thousand-square-foot home. According to Shelly, "The screening room and bowling alley took up a lot of space, so the house really didn't feel as big as it sounds." More importantly, though, Shelly wasn't feeling satisfied. With a newborn and a brand-new home to enjoy, her days continued to be spent on planning and attending fund-raisers and accompanying Seth on his business engagements. They had a second daughter, Lucy. And still, life continued as it had before. Paying for additional support staff for their growing family was never an issue; her two daughters were now a part of their jet-set life, nannies and all. And then she became pregnant again with daughter number three, Rachel.

The nonstop travel, social engagements, and "utter exhausting craziness" continued for several more years until Shelly hit a wall. Her dissatisfaction with her life had turned to misery. She hadn't made any real friends in years—only acquaintances who were in need of her time and money—and she had no time to do anything for herself. She wasn't as involved a parent as she always thought she'd be because she was too busy fulfilling the various social obligations that had ceased being important to her. In her heart, she felt as if she had thrown away ten years of her life.

At that point, Shelly made an unusual decision and followed through using pretty drastic measures: She chose to downscale her life and start over. She sold her house, pulled her eldest daughters (Allison and Lucy) out of private school, and withdrew her name from every charity and committee she had joined. She bought a smaller home, enrolled all three girls in public school, and began walking them over each day. Instead of planning soirees, she began to plan school bake sales and other PTA events. No more gala gowns and jewelry, just jeans and T-shirts. She wanted to get to know her kids, meet real people, and live a fuller but simpler life before it was too late. Seth supported the decision. He wanted her to be happy. And as long as he had his professional empire and his wife by his side, he was content. When I met Shelly, this revised lifestyle had been in place for about four months. She was practicing yoga more consistently, reconnecting with old friends, and starting to feel like "the old Shelly."

Her kids, though, were another story. Lucy and Allison hated their new life. They missed vacationing in Hawaii and the weekend shopping trips with mom. They made fun of Shelly's new hybrid car and wondered what had happened to the Range Rover. Four-year-old Rachel, still in preschool, seemed to be taking it all in stride. Shelly was deeply disappointed in the older girls' attitude. As far as she was concerned, Lucy and Allison were still clothed, fed, and loved, and that should've been enough.

> *Shelly: What is wrong with them? Can't they see how lucky they are?*
>
> *Dr. Sophy: Have you seen any other changes in them?*
>
> *Shelly: Like what?*
>
> *Dr. Sophy: How's their sleeping?*
>
> *Shelly: Actually, not so great. It may be they're still not used to their new bedroom or something, but give me a break, it's still a nice room.*
>
> *Dr. Sophy: Anything else going on? Any problems at school?*
>
> *Shelly: Not really . . . except that Allison's teacher mentioned the other day that she looked sad during recess and thought it had interfered with her spelling test later that day.*

At this point I had to leave, yet I hadn't had much of a chance to respond or offer any guidance. But clearly, there was a lot going on with this family. I suggested that Shelly come to see me with

her two eldest daughters, and we made an appointment for the following week. I thought it best to see them together. I had a pretty
good sense of Shelly at this point, and wanted to meet Lucy and
Allison and see how they interacted sooner rather later.

Shelly, Lucy, and Allison

The day of the appointment, neither daughter was speaking to
Shelly. I could tell that the powerful tension of the back-to-back
position between mom and her daughters was uncomfortable for
all of them. The girls looked angry, both with fierce green eyes.
Shelly looked at me with embarrassment. Though common, it was
frustrating for me to see the incredible amount of energy that was
being wasted on creating this stance when the same energy could
be used to create a solid face-to-face position that would eventually lead to side-by-side.

They walked into my office, and the seating arrangement happened naturally. It was also quite perfect. Allison and Lucy sat
next to each other in the two chairs; mom sat on the couch across
from them. In this way, mom was in a literal face-to-face position
with both girls. I sat at my desk, a third-party observer of this
group. I began by explaining to them that the point of coming
together was so they could talk. I also told them briefly about the
Chair Strategy, explained the three positions, and then pointed
out that the way they had naturally sat down had significance.
You could see understanding on their faces. Then I shared the
Rules of Talking:

1. Respect each other by listening.

2. Do not speak when the other is speaking.

3. Let the other person finish, even if you disagree.

4. Choose the established signal that lets the other person
   know you would like to talk.

Shelly asked to speak first.

> Shelly: I am so glad we're here. Dr. Sophy, I've been trying to explain to my girls why there's been a change in our lifestyle. The bottom line for me is that money really is poison. They just don't understand this concept.

> Lucy: Since when is money poison, Mom? Since you said it is?

Although Lucy was the younger sister, it was clear that she spoke for both of them, as her sister seemed quite shy.

> Shelly: OK, maybe poison is a strong word, but you know what I mean. We just don't need all those material things to make us happy.

> Lucy: That's your opinion. Plus it's not just "things" to us, Mom.

> Shelly: I wish you could understand what a wonderful change this is, Lucy and Ally. How can I help them see this, Dr. Sophy?

> Dr. Sophy: It is my job to listen right now and ask questions. Lucy, what did you mean when you said, "It's not just 'things' to us?"

> Lucy: I miss my friends. This new school is just wrong. I mean, I'm sure the people are OK, but why do I have to be there?

> Shelly: Why can't you just trust that I'm making a good decision for all of us? I'm your mother!

No one said anything. Shelly's leg began to twirl and kick as before. Lucy had a very good point, and one that clearly hadn't been addressed.

> Dr. Sophy: Lucy, when you think about money, what does it make you feel, I mean, in your heart?

She was silent for a moment.

Lucy: Wow, no one's ever asked me a question like that before. That's weird.

Dr. Sophy: It's called connecting your head to your heart. This is something we should all be doing right now. Close your eyes a moment and think about a favorite memory from your old life. Allison and Shelly, you do the same, please.

The three of them closed their eyes.

Dr. Sophy: Let's go around and talk about how we feel when we think about that old life.

Shelly: I'll start. It makes me feel miserable . . . empty . . . lonely . . . tired . . . depressed.

Lucy and Allison were silent. I could see both of them were getting emotional, still with eyes closed.

Lucy: When I think about that old life and all that money, I feel . . .

She struggled to stay composed.

Shelly: Why are you crying? Dr. Sophy, why is she crying?

Dr. Sophy: Please, Shelly, give Lucy a moment. (Then) How do you feel when you think of money?

Lucy: Like I'm loved. I feel good. I feel real good.

Lucy began to cry. As Allison nodded her head in agreement, she began to cry as well.

Shelly: Why do you think that? What does that mean, Dr. Sophy?

Allison: It just feels like you don't love us anymore, Mom.

As her body started to relax a bit, I could see that Shelly was beginning to understand. All their lives, Lucy and Allison had equated love with material objects, and these things had connected the whole family, the three females in particular. This family had placed a high value on their possessions and what they could buy. For them, the importance of all the trips and goods they had acquired was not that they had done so *together* but that they had actually taken those particular trips or purchased those items. Now that those items were taken away, in their minds, love was taken from them as well. Connecting their head to their heart was the beginning of their recovery process. For the first time, mom could understand how difficult this downsizing was for her daughters—not because they were brats or spoiled, but because they felt lost and unloved. And her daughters finally felt understood by mom. The tight bond Lucy and Allison once had with their mom was based on activities related to spending money, such as shopping, going out to eat, and traveling. They were mourning the loss of this connection to their mom.

As Shelly had begun to fulfill her newfound desire to be whole and grounded in a different way, she forgot one important task—to communicate with her kids about this shift in her priorities and actions. She was so wrapped up in her own needs that she neglected to explain to them why the ground had shifted. Although her efforts were intended to make her girls better off in the long run, Lucy and Allison remained clueless as to how this was possible because mom approached this change in a back-to-back way rather than in an open, face-to-face dialogue. It was now up to Shelly to let her daughters know why she decided to drastically alter her family's lifestyle. (Of course, if this family's values were clearer, this self-imposed downsizing would have been experienced in a much different and more positive way.)

With this family, there was a large amount of what I often refer to as undoing work that needed to be done. Because the values they embraced had been superficial, they needed essentially to have a redo and start over, especially because of their major lifestyle change in the last year. I suggested weekly family therapy for this family, with dad included, so that I could more effectively help them weave together their thoughts and feelings and guide their transition to this new life.

Aside from these weekly sessions, some of their initial treatment plan included:

- *Family meetings at home.* Each week, the family (both parents and all three girls) had a specific meeting place (they chose the family room) where they discussed issues that arose—anything from school activities and mom's yoga class to the new medical breakthrough dad was working on. Each had time to share a topic.

- *Guided Journaling.* At the beginning of each family meeting, everyone read aloud his or her journal entries that had been written in response to the previous week's assignment. Rachel would draw pictures, as she wasn't writing yet. The topic of the entry was chosen by someone different each week and was generally based on an issue related to the move, such as the new school, what they missed most about their old life, or a family memory.

- *Weekly exercise—walking or biking.* The group of five spent forty-five minutes each week doing some kind of outdoor activity together. It was a wonderful way for them to connect.

- *Chair Strategy.* After this family began to show significant signs of improvement, they learned the Chair Strategy.

The untraditional nature of this family—downsizing by choice—brings up so many of the same issues as downsizing due to necessity. As the following story illustrates, though issues of money may vary widely among families, it is the value system that must remain the foundation of a family.

The Money Talk

A fourteen-year-old daughter pushes a cart at a Target store as mom pulls items from the shelves and drops them in. Their cart is full of household necessities such as cleaning solution, paper towels, and laundry detergent. Mom takes a dress from the clothing rack and adds it to the pile in the cart.

Daughter: That dress is so ugly.

Mom: Hey, you need something to wear to church.

Daughter: OK, but I want this one.

The daughter takes another dress off the rack. Mom grabs it out of her hands and looks at the price tag.

Mom: It's too expensive. Put it back.

The daughter rolls her eyes and hesitates.

Mom: No attitude. Put it back now!

Daughter: Unbelievable!

Mom: Tell me about it.

Defeated, the daughter returns her dress of choice to the rack. She eyes the ugly dress that remains in her basket, knowing she'll be wearing it to church every Sunday for the entire year. Her eyes soften.

Daughter: How come I . . .

Mom: Shut up, OK? You're lucky to get any dress.

Rather than deal with her daughter's requested face-to-face discussion, this mom opted for a back-to-back stance and missed a perfect opportunity to initiate a discussion on money and values. This interaction may have stirred up several issues for mom—feeling like a failure because she could not fulfill her daughter's simple

Values: The Tooth Fairy

The idea of the tooth fairy is a perfect way to start a conversation with your young daughter about values. As you help her place her tooth under the pillow, talk about what she can expect. Will the tooth fairy bring money? How much will it be—a nickel, a quarter, or even a dollar? Some other kind of gift? Or will the tooth fairy leave a note? Along with your spouse, you will decide, of course, what is appropriate for the tooth fairy to bring. Whatever that may be, it will surely stay in your daughter's memory forever. (And remember, her expectation may be that the tooth fairy will be coming back nineteen more times!)

request, resentment that her daughter expected to be taken care of when no one was taking care of her, and a general reminder of their daily struggle with money. Regardless of the reason, honest and respectful communication could have gone a long way toward drawing these two closer. The strong reactions that both of them had to the dress—the emotions that put them in a back-to-back position—were exactly the kind of passion needed to work through the conflict.

I am often asked if a parent's money issues affect the children and, if so, should they be discussed with them? The simple answers are yes and yes. Everything that affects you affects your children. And there is no question that if one or both parents have lost a job or are facing a decrease in income, the kids will know it. You must let your family know what is going on. The questions are: How much should the children know? At what age? The answers are different for every family. However, here are some general guidelines:

- Listen. Listen. Listen. What your child asks or says about money is a great indication of where she is with it both emotionally and developmentally. Listen to what she has to say.

- Pay attention to your own emotions, and try to remain neutral when discussing the subject with her. She is more perceptive than you realize.

- Explain concepts related to both money and values.

- Establish guidelines. Kids need this, especially when it comes to money. Start by giving your child an allowance that is contingent upon the completion of chores or good deeds.

- Walk the walk. If you tell her "No more new DVDs" because you're trying to save money, stick to it—and don't come home loaded down with shopping bags.

The discussion of money and values is not a one-time event; rather, it should be an ongoing discussion. No matter what you choose to teach your daughter through your words and actions, the most important point is to begin the conversation with a focus on values and in a face-to-face position. The more you can instill within her solid values, the stronger she will be, regardless of the economic circumstance she may face. Money comes and goes. Values are hers to keep forever.

EXERCISE: WANTS VERSUS NEEDS

I encourage my patients to clarify their issues regarding money and values by this simple journaling exercise. It can be a fun and informative activity for you and your daughter to do together. Why not give it a try?

Turn to a clean page in your journal. Draw a line down the center of the page. Label one side: "Things I Want That Are Valuable to Me," and label the other side: "Things I Want That Cost Money." Here's an example of a list from a forty-five-year-old mom:

Things I Want That Are Valuable to Me	Things I Want That Cost Money
1. Spending Christmas with my parents	1. Flat-screen TV
2. Seeing college friends	2. Highlights in my hair
3. College education for my children	3. College education for my children
4. For my kids to feel safe	4. A new car—any kind, just new!
5. Family dinners three nights a week	5. Dressy wristwatch

Evaluation: Questions to Consider

If you've done this activity alone:

- Notice if anything is the same for both headings (e.g., #3 above, "college education"). Here something valuable costs money, and the reverse is also true.

- Are you able to obtain your valuable wants?

- Are you able to afford your wants that cost money?

If you've done this activity with your daughter, ask the same questions as above and add:

- Do your lists have anything in common?

This chapter has explored the money-and-value system within a family. Our next hot-button issue to explore is divorce, which ironically is often triggered by money issues. Though this connection will not be our focus, it is interesting to note how these heated issues influence each other.

Divorce

OUTSIDE A COFFEE SHOP, early on a Saturday morning, a middle-aged woman and her teenage daughter are having a heated discussion in the parking lot. Their faces are angry, and their arms are wildly gesturing. Several minutes later, they embrace tightly. Both are weeping. An SUV pulls up next to them and parks; a middle-aged man gets out. The two women pull apart and greet him.

Young Woman: Hi, Daddy.

Mother: Hello, Michael.

Father: Hi, Jane. (Turning to the teenager) Hey, Sandy . . . ya ready?

Young Woman: Yep, I'll get my stuff. (Then) Love you, Mom.

Mom: Love you too, Sandy.

Sandy grabs a small suitcase out of mom's car. Dad gets out of the SUV and makes small talk with his ex-wife. Dad's passenger car door opens; a skimpily dressed thirty-something woman gets out and possessively attaches herself to dad. Mom struggles for composure as she engages in friendly small talk with dad's new girlfriend. Sandy throws her suitcase into dad's car. Dad, his girl-friend, and Sandy get into the car. Mom waves good-bye as they drive off. Then she gets into her car and drives away.

The weekend child exchange of divorced parents is the reality for roughly half of all families in America. And within my private practice, families of divorce account for over half of my regular patients. Of those, 75 percent are mothers and daughters. As with the other hot-button issues we have addressed, there are basic triggers that make divorce an emotionally charged experience, regardless of the specifics of the family. But nothing tests the strength of the mother-daughter relationship like divorce. More than any other issue, divorce causes a mom to question her identity as a woman and as a mom. In turn, these feelings can easily and significantly cloud the communication between mother and daughter, both consciously and subconsciously, which can interfere with their relationship in general.

Aside from the emotional shifts within the family unit during divorce, there are oftentimes structural or environmental changes as well, such as alterations in living situations, daily routines, even schools. These changes may begin well before and will certainly continue long after the actual divorce. As these events unfold, it is key that mother and daughter continue to communicate effectively and in a face-to-face position. This communication is extremely challenging even for a mom who has diligently done her up-front work and is armed with strength, balance, and clarity.

A divorce will test even the healthiest mother-daughter relationships. You now have (in addition to your strength, balance, and clarity) the Chair Strategy to guide you through this extremely difficult and life-altering event. Divorce changes all family members indelibly. And whether you were the one who initiated the divorce or were dragged into it, you are responsible for guiding your daughter through it.

The dissolution of a marriage may legally sever the bond between husband and wife, but emotionally these bonds may never be severed. A divorce means the end of an intimate relationship for mom. Even if that relationship was actually over long before the official divorce decree or separation agreement, there's a different finality once those papers are signed. Mom's second *E* in S.W.E.E.P., her emotional expression of self, has been altered.

The complication for mom is that after a divorce, her relationship with her ex-husband changes not just physically but emotionally. The relationship must be redefined, and in many ways, mom must pull back from dad in order to stay strong, balanced, and clear. At the same time, unless dad is dangerous, daughter's relationship with her dad (mom's ex-husband) must continue to flourish emotionally. Part of mom's job is to support her daughter through this process so that her daughter stays connected to dad—the very man she is trying to disconnect from. This man will always be the father of her daughter and, as such, whether mom wants to accept it or not, her daughter *needs* to have her father involved in her life for the sake of her emotional development. So mom must be committed to this effort even though dad may very well be someone she can no longer be in the same room with or, worse yet, someone with whom she is still deeply in love. This residual feeling is what oftentimes determines the communication path that mom takes with her daughter.

Throughout this book, we've stressed the importance of honest communication and being authentic and clear about who you are. A divorce will put all of this to the test, in part because the rules change. They have to. Why? Because during divorce there are many issues going on between you and your ex-partner that simply cannot be discussed with complete honesty with your daughter. There's no appropriate way to tell her, for example, that your ex is a disgusting, unfaithful dirtbag. And let's face it: Any age-appropriate solutions you come up with to convey these messages will *not* be appropriate. How could they be? This is one of those times when a mom just has to suck it up, even if she has diligently done her up-front work.

To add to the challenge, her daughter may very well be a conscious or subconscious reminder of the man she is divorcing. In some cases, the daughter may even look like a carbon copy of the offending character. The same big brown eyes, winning smile, and adorable dimple—the very traits that once made mom swoon—now make her sick to her stomach. And still, she must meet the challenge and connect her head with her heart in a balanced way so that she communicates appropriately with her daughter throughout the divorce process. Further, divorce and perceived transfer of sexuality can be intertwined; recall Stephanie and her nineteen-year-old daughter, Liza, who were featured in the chapter on sex. Part of mom's perceived transfer of sexuality was due to her feelings of inadequacy after the breakup of her marriage. More importantly, Truth #4 (mothers and daughters, on some level, are in competition with each other) can be most evident during a divorce. No wonder navigating through a divorce is so difficult!

The conscious or subconscious communication choices mom makes—whether they are to protect her daughter or to rely on her for support—are full of intense emotion. Therefore, these choices often result in exactly the opposite of the desired outcome. In essence, mom must encourage her daughter to express herself as much as possible while she herself is not afforded the same luxury. In my experience, a mom in the midst of divorce usually chooses one of the two following paths of communication with her daughter:

1. In order to protect her daughter from her pain, mom shares very little with her daughter and keeps her at arm's length. As a result, the daughter naturally feels alone, confused, and lost. And for mom, the shutdown of her S.W.E.E.P.'s second *E*—emotional expression of self—toward her daughter on anything related to the divorce can come out in other ways, such as imposing strict rules, having no patience for her daughter, or showing disrespect toward her. Additionally, if mom has any subconscious or unresolved resentment toward her daughter's blossoming relationship with dad, you can see how this may add fuel to the PTS fire.

2. In order to garner emotional support for herself, mom enlists daughter as an ally or companion and shares way too much information by treating her daughter like a buddy. She may even regale her with inappropriate details about the divorce and unkind stories about dad. In the short-term, this approach may interfere with daughter's relationship with her dad. In the long term, it will damage the relationship between mother and daughter.

When a mom makes the first choice during a divorce, she has essentially taken a back-to-back position with her daughter. Though withholding her own sadness and pain from her daughter may feel like a loving decision, this is not the case. How could it be? How can a daughter—while experiencing what may be the most difficult time in her own life—feel loved, understood, or respected when her mom has shut her out emotionally?

When a mom makes the second choice, she has gone in the opposite but equally unhealthy direction. In some ways, mom has committed to an unnatural side-by-side position with her daughter by making her a pal. This is not a position that any daughter wants to be in or that a mom should place her daughter in.

Tanya and Grace

People all over the country send me questions after checking out my Web site, and I respond to each one. Though I can't diagnose or treat anyone online, of course, I am able to offer advice and to direct him or her toward the appropriate health care professionals.

Here is one of the e-mails I received:

Dear Dr. Sophy:

I need help with my seven-year-old daughter. She is having an MRI scan next week because of headaches she has been having. I've never had an MRI scan myself, but everyone tells me they can be intimidating, particularly for a young child. What is the best way to prepare her so that she is not scared? I've been told that I

can't stay in the room with her, so I'm extra nervous about this.
Please give me any advice you have.

Thanks,

Tanya

I wrote back to Tanya to gather a bit more information. From her response I learned that her daughter, Grace, had only recently been having headaches, but they seemed to be very painful. Their pediatrician didn't seem concerned, so Tanya sought a second opinion. The new pediatrician, though also not alarmed, suggested an eye exam and a blood test. Both of these tests showed no indication of anything serious, which was definitely good news. Just to be safe, though, he ordered an MRI as an extra precaution. Because they lived just outside of Los Angeles, Tanya asked if I could see Grace before the MRI, which I was happy to do. In the interest of time, I asked both Tanya and Grace to come to the initial visit. And I told her I needed to connect with the pediatrician before our appointment to find out any more pertinent medical information.

When I spoke to the pediatrician, he told me that Grace's headaches had started two months before. They seemed to be at their worst, according to mom, on Sunday nights after the girl's weekly softball game. The physician reiterated that the MRI was a precautionary measure and felt that the headaches were probably caused by the physical activity of playing softball. I asked if he had seen any records from the original pediatrician, and if so was there any kind of medical history of note? He mentioned that two years earlier Grace had experienced several months of stomach problems but none of the tests had turned up anything serious. Though I knew very little about Grace at this point, I had the feeling there was more to these headaches than just a physical condition.

Tanya and Grace came to see me on a Friday afternoon, arriving fifteen minutes late to the appointment. Before I could get any kind of greeting out, an aggravated and apologetic Tanya explained their tardiness: "I had to get this one packed up for the weekend with dad, you know how that goes . . ."

I turned to Grace and smiled. She smiled back sweetly.

Grace: I'm thirsty. Do you have any juice?

Mom: Grace! (Then) Dr. Sophy, just water for her if you have it, please.

Dr. Sophy: You're in luck! I do have juice.

Grace: What kind of juice?

Mom: Stop it, Grace!

Dr. Sophy: It's OK, Tanya, really. (Then to Grace) Apple?

Grace smiled and gave me the thumbs-up. I grabbed a juice box (I always keep a few around for kids) and handed it to Grace. At that point, I explained to Grace that her mom and I would spend some time in my office privately, while she stayed in the waiting area. She was more than happy with that idea. She had her juice, and she could see that the waiting room had some pretty fun stuff to play with. Grace was a very confident and competent seven-year-old.

Once Tanya and I had privacy in my office, I asked her about the weekend with dad. She explained that she was divorced from Grace's dad, Bob, and this was his weekend to care for her. She was quick to add: "Not that he knows the first thing about what *care* means. He's a total loser." Tanya explained to me that their initial connection was purely physical and, if she was completely honest with herself, she knew even on that first date there was not a chance for anything more than that. Bob had shown up late, taken her to a "cheap restaurant," and, to top it off, needed her help changing a flat tire on the way home. But his dimples won out, and they ended up in bed on that first date. Second date, same thing, only this time she got pregnant. She married him quickly thereafter. Big mistake. By the time Grace was four, Bob had fallen in love with another woman and Tanya, upon discovering this, promptly kicked him out of the house. She told me, "Honestly, it was the happiest day of my life."

Regardless of Bob's actions, Tanya's extremely vocal and negative attitude toward her ex-husband was so close to the surface, I could only imagine what Grace had been privy to. And though the short-term priority here was to get Grace through this MRI, it was clear to me that Tanya needed a lot of help to appropriately deal with her divorce. She clearly had not done so.

Before we discussed the plans for Grace's MRI, I asked Tanya to tell me more about Grace's day-to-day life so I could figure out how best to approach her about the upcoming test. Tanya explained that she and Grace had lived on their own for about two years since she divorced her husband. She took this as another opportunity to bash Bob, describing him as "nasty, selfish, and the worst dad on the planet." I asked her if he was abusive in any way toward either of them and she replied: "Nope, that would take too much energy. Bob's a lazy slob." She explained that he barely made time for Grace until just recently. He now took her one weekend a month as well as every Sunday from three to five p.m. This was the plan they had worked out. Tanya's attitude toward Bob continued to illustrate the profound back-to-back position that Grace had been witnessing between her mom and her dad.

I asked Tanya about their Sundays, as I knew this was when Grace's headaches seemed to be at their worst. Typically they went to church in the morning, had lunch with friends, and then, most recently, Grace and dad played softball in the afternoon. After that, Tanya picked up Grace from the park, the two of them had dinner out, then went back home for the night. Tanya noted that these headaches had gotten so painful that she and Grace hadn't been able to have their ritual girls' night. I asked her what girls' night was. She explained that for the last several months, every Sunday night they would give each other manicures and chat. It had started one Sunday after Grace had come home from the weekend with Bob and seemed sad. To cheer her up, Tanya suggested they have a girls' night.

Dr. Sophy: What kinds of things do you talk about?

Tanya: Whatever is on her mind or my mind. Really, anything.

Dr Sophy: Do the two of you talk about Bob on girls' night?

Tanya: Of course! Wouldn't be girls' night without him for laughs!

Dr. Sophy: Does Grace seem to miss girls' night?

Tanya: I'm sure she does, but what can we do? By the time I get out the nail polish, her head is starting to really hurt.

I knew at this point that girls' night was not a good thing, as it involved inappropriate talk about Grace's dad. Tanya had turned Grace into her divorce buddy. I had a strong suspicion that Grace felt uncomfortable and that this ritual, in some way, could very well be the reason she was having these headaches. It was a conscious or subconscious way for Grace to get out of having to engage with mom in negative talk about dad (in order to make mom feel good).

At this point, I asked her about the stomach problems Grace had had a few years ago. Tanya remembered it only vaguely, but did recall that it was during the time she and Bob were first splitting up. She told me, "There was so much going on." She and Bob were fighting like cats and dogs, he was in the process of moving out, and, on top of everything else, Grace was having tummy-aches. It turned out to be nothing that over-the-counter medications couldn't treat.

Our time was running out, and I had not yet gotten a chance to address the issue of the MRI. I also didn't have enough time to explain to mom exactly what I believed to be the cause of these headaches. What I did do was tell mom that I wanted to bring Grace into the room and to tell her that Sunday girls' night was officially over. Instead, on Sunday nights after dinner they would do an activity such as water coloring, playing with clay, or cooking . . . if Grace felt up to it. On Sunday, when Tanya would pick up Grace from playing with Bob, she should remind her of the plan and try it out (provided there's no headache). If they did begin the activity, the conversation should be about the activity itself, not about trashing other people, particularly Bob, who was, after all, Grace's dad. In the meantime, I told Tanya I would like to call the pediatrician and see if it would be OK to postpone the MRI for another week so I could see Grace one more time beforehand. Tanya agreed and was relieved to have the extra week. She had no idea, though, about the real work she had ahead of her. Plan in motion, mom went to get Grace from the waiting room.

She had drawn a picture to bring to her dad; she proudly showed mom.

Grace: What do you think?

Though she tried hard to cover it, I could see the resentment on Tanya's face over the fact that Bob was getting anything so precious from his daughter. And competent Grace could sense something as well.

Grace: It's OK?

Tanya: (A bit forced) Your picture is beautiful.

Grace: Thanks, but . . . I mean . . . it's OK if I give it to Daddy?

Tanya: Of course, why wouldn't it be?

It was clear how much Grace knew about her mom's unkind feelings toward dad. I told Tanya to tell Grace what we had discussed.

Tanya: Listen, I have an idea for something you and I could do Sunday night after I pick you up from the park.

I could see Grace bristle at the words *Sunday night.*

Tanya: Why don't we go over to that pottery place or bake something special?

Grace: Really? That sounds fun.

Plan in motion, we said our good-byes, and I told Tanya to call me on Sunday night after Grace had gone to sleep to give me an update. As I suspected, when she checked in on Sunday, Tanya reported no headache from Grace—the first time in seven consecutive Sunday nights that she didn't have one. Tanya was stunned.

On Monday morning, I called the pediatrician. I shared this new information, and he agreed with me that these headaches were more than likely brought on by anxiety or tension. I suspected it was the latter, a tension headache. He felt that the MRI could be postponed and probably wasn't necessary at all, at least not until I had one more session with Grace and Tanya. (There have been many cases where I have seen children of divorce exhibit mysterious symptoms that proved to be either manufactured for attention or psychosomatic.)

Several days later, the two of them returned to my office. With confidence, Grace walked in, requested apple juice, and told mom and me, "I'll be in the waiting room if you need me." I explained to her that this time she would be joining us in the other room. She was more than happy to comply. We all sat down, and I asked Grace to tell me about the pottery she made on Sunday night with her mom. Eyes wide with excitement, she filled me in:

Grace: I painted a bowl all by myself! With stars and a heart, so pretty!

Tanya: It was really beautiful, Dr. Sophy. It will be ready to pick up this week. I even made a bowl!

Mom looked toward me for approval; she was so proud of herself. I nodded and smiled.

Dr. Sophy: What a fun night you two had! Imagine when you can eat cereal or ice cream in those bowls together.

Tanya: Great idea. (To Grace) Let's have an ice cream party next Sunday night!

Grace was quiet, and suddenly looked very sad.

Dr. Sophy: What are you thinking about, Grace?

Grace: Dad . . . He doesn't have a bowl. Can we go back there on Sunday night and make one for him?

Tanya: But what about our ice cream party?

There it was, Tanya's jealousy and resentment oozing out. Grace said nothing. All of mom's dad-bashing had pushed her daughter closer to her dad, rather than giving mom an ally. Of course, it's good for daughter to feel closer to dad, but not with that as the catalyst. I gave Tanya a look. She knew what she had said and had to concede.

Tanya: Yes, we can make dad a bowl. Of course we can.

Grace: Thanks!

At this point, I asked Grace to go back in the waiting room while her mom and I talked some more. She left without complaint.

Tanya: So, what are we thinking about this whole MRI business?

Dr. Sophy: Honestly, I don't think she needs one. I believe her headaches are caused from stress and tension about the fact that you and Bob have an unresolved situation. She understands a lot more than you realize.

Tanya: What does she understand? What do you mean exactly?

Dr. Sophy: Let's start with this. Tell me how you feel when you think about helping Grace make a bowl for Bob.

Tanya: Disgusted. Why on earth would I want to make a bowl for him?

Dr. Sophy: OK, fair enough. What do you think that means?

Tanya: That I hate him, because I do. I hate him.

Dr. Sophy: Do you know what the opposite of love is?

Tanya: Of course I do. Hate.

Dr. Sophy: No, actually the opposite of love is neutrality.

Tanya: So, what are you saying?

*Dr. Sophy: That you clearly still have strong feelings for Bob—
even though they are negative. We need to work through this so
you can get to a more neutral place for both yourself and for the
health of your daughter.*

I explained to Tanya that the real focus of our work together
was to navigate through her feelings about Bob and the divorce.
By doing this, and getting clear, she would be freer to allow Grace's
relationship with Bob to grow and, in turn, everyone would benefit. As it stood, Tanya was making it difficult for Grace to feel comfortable to connect with her dad. This had to stop; Grace needed
to feel safe to love him.

Generally speaking, I am not the kind of couch psychiatrist
who spends six months on the kind of work Tanya needed. I give
my patients concrete tools so that their recovery can get started
immediately. In fact, one of the reasons I had suggested that she
literally help make a bowl for Bob is that the physical process of
doing something for him would jump-start her healing process.
She needed to do it because it was important to Grace, regardless of how it made her feel. It was time that Tanya placed herself
firmly in a face-to-face position with Grace in all communications
regarding dad. And once this happened (it already had started), I
was certain that Grace's headaches—her own version of the back-
to-back stance—would truly be a problem of the past.

Before Tanya and Grace left that day, Tanya committed to work-
ing with me for a couple of months in order to get her life in order.
For her, it was more a job of undoing rather than up-front work.
Here's what we did.

Treatment Plan for Tanya and Grace

Mom's undoing work included everything you've done in your own up-front work with a few variations:

- The First Look exercise. I encouraged her to pay special attention to Bob's role in Grace's birth and to focus on something positive that he offered during the pregnancy and birthing process.

- The Four Truths, with special attention to Truth #1: Mothers and daughters want the same things: love, understanding, and respect (the cornerstone). The idea that Tanya and Grace both needed these things, particularly where the divorce was concerned, was key.

- S.W.E.E.P., with special attention to the second *E*. This was the part of mom's life that had changed most drastically and needed the biggest boost.

- The idea of Grace as an opportunity was even more layered now. Because Grace was watching Tanya so closely (as all daughters do with their moms), she was learning so much from her during this divorce about the relationships between men and women. Tanya needed to pay special attention to this.

- Mom began a journal, starting with her unmet needs list, and continued with her thoughts on her life as a single mom.

- Grace also began a journal, which she was to take with her even to dad's house for those weekends with him. In this journal, Grace would write or draw or place stickers— basically, however she chose to express herself.

- Sunday nights were reestablished as mom/daughter night, and they would take turns choosing the activity.

Fran and Roslyn

Fran came to see me several months after her college graduation. She was a striking young woman, tall and thin with green eyes, shoulder-length red hair, and an appealing freckled complexion. She began our initial meeting by telling me about her upcoming move to New York City to begin an advertising job. Moving to the city was an idea she'd always had in the back of her mind, and she was thrilled with the opportunity she'd been handed. Fran had actually lived there until the age of three, at which time her parents divorced and she and her mom moved back to Los Angeles. Since her mom's entire family lived in California, her mom had felt this would be the best place to raise Fran. Her dad was an international businessman who traveled a lot but whose main residence was in Manhattan. For most of her life, Fran had only seen her dad once or twice a year when he passed through Los Angeles, yet she felt very close to him. At this point, dad's traveling had slowed down, and he was spending more and more time in Manhattan.

Aside from being able to take advantage of this incredible job opportunity, the move to New York would allow her to reconnect with her dad. She had also been offered a job in Los Angeles and had been considering both. When Fran told her mom she accepted the job in New York over the one in Los Angeles, her mom got very upset and questioned why she would move so far away when there was an opportunity close by. Fran told her mom, in all honesty, that both jobs were equally appealing but moving to the East Coast would give her the chance to reconnect with her dad. At this point, mom became enraged and shouted, "That man couldn't care less about you. Don't you see that? He will break your heart!"

Though Fran understood her mom's reaction, she felt certain that moving to New York was the right choice for her. As our session wound down, I asked if she thought her mom would come in with her. We scheduled for the following week, planning a joint session for Fran and her mom.

The following week, Fran showed up alone and extremely upset. She told me that her mom refused to come to therapy and at that point had completely stopped speaking to her. We spent the session talking about her life with mom and without dad. Fran told me that dad was simply someone who didn't exist in their family. Her mom literally never mentioned him. But then every time Fran would see him—which was not that often—she recalled feeling really connected to him. To her, it almost didn't matter that they spent such little time together because she always felt his presence.

Fran remembers telling her mother this when she was about eight years old and they were having a quiet dinner together at the beach. Her mother said nothing in response. Thinking that she hadn't heard, Fran repeated the statement. "I heard you the first time," her mom replied, and then changed the subject. That was the last time she had any memory of talking to her mom about her dad—until now. Fran knew that her mom had no interest in sharing with her the details of the painful divorce. And now that Fran was an adult, she wanted to pursue her own relationship with her dad, despite the fact that her mother was so deeply hurt by him. Fran was one brave young woman.

Though I didn't know her mom, I explained to Fran that many women cope with divorce by shutting down emotionally. It sounded like this was what her mom had done. And because there was very little communication regarding her mother's feelings about dad and the divorce in general, Fran had very little to go on. Based on mom's reaction to Fran's leaving, it was clear that mom was still hurting because she had never dealt with her own feelings about dad and the fact that he was no longer in her life. And it was more than possible that mom was jealous and resentful of Fran because she had the opportunity to reconnect with this man with whom she was probably still in love. Mom's response to Fran, upon hearing the news of her pending move, seemed to be a projection of her own hurt: "That man couldn't care less about you. Don't you see that? He will break your heart!" It all made sense to

Fran. I urged her to continue reaching out to her mom with calls, e-mails, whatever it took. And to try her hardest to see her before she moved to New York.

Without meeting her mom, I couldn't be certain, but it seemed to me that the attitude she'd exhibited toward her ex was for loving reasons, mainly to protect her daughter. It was as if mom thought she was taking a side-by-side stance on the issue of dad, when in reality her behavior was a classic back-to-back posture that caused even more pain and confusion. While I was also disappointed that Fran's mom hadn't come in with her, several weeks later I was thrilled when she called to schedule an appointment.

Statuesque but extremely timid, Roslyn nervously walked into my office. She had short gray hair and a beautiful smile. The minute she sat down, she was fighting tears. I told her how happy I was that she had decided to come in, and how wonderful I thought Fran was. That was when she started to cry.

> *Roslyn: Yes, Fran is wonderful. And I always thought I was doing the right thing with her, always.*
>
> *Dr. Sophy: What do you mean?*
>
> *Roslyn: I tried to shield her, that's what I thought moms were supposed to do.*

Roslyn explained to me how devastated she was when Alex, Fran's dad, had asked for a divorce. It had come out of nowhere. At the time they had been together for seven years and been married for five, and she was completely blindsided. He simply wanted out of the marriage and gave no real explanation. His job was extremely time-consuming, including lots of travel, and he felt it was best not even to try to make it work. Alex gave Roslyn no choice in the matter. So she packed her bags and moved back home to Los Angeles within a week. Though he told her he loved their daughter, he simply didn't have the time to put into the relationship and would be OK with having a minimal presence in Fran's life.

Roslyn: So there you have it. The love of my life, gone.

Dr. Sophy: Does Fran know that he was the love of your life?

Roslyn: Of course not. Why would she know that?

This fact was actually a positive, something that Fran would have truly benefited from knowing. Instead, she was led to believe that there had never been any love between them. Roslyn's feelings of abandonment caused her to react as she did regarding her husband and now, once again, Roslyn felt she was being abandoned—this time by her own daughter. It was more than she could handle.

Roslyn: I don't what to do at this point. Please help me.

She began to cry.

Dr. Sophy: I have to tell you, Roslyn, that from what you've just told me, you have begun to help yourself.

Roslyn: How is that possible?

Dr. Sophy: You started with the truth, the feelings you had about Alex. When's the last time you've actually talked about the fact that you ever loved him?

Roslyn: Years. Decades.

Dr. Sophy: Truth is good, Roslyn.

She was quiet.

Roslyn: I'd like to talk to Fran. She tried many times to reach me before she left, but I didn't respond. She'll probably never speak to me again.

I told Roslyn that this simply wasn't true; Fran loved her and would stop at nothing to reconnect. We agreed to try to set up a conference call for the three of us, which did happen the following week. Before the call, Roslyn and I had one more session.

We talked about the importance of her embracing the relationship that Fran was developing with her dad. The more Fran felt safe to express herself about dad, the better connection mom and daughter would have. Mom's support of this relationship was key to repairing the slightly damaged one she now had with Fran.

Roslyn was beginning to understand. Her residual feelings toward dad, though she'd thought she covered them so well, had left her an emotional shell of a woman, the mom Fran knew and still loved very much. Roslyn was beginning to see that—for her own benefit as well as her relationship with her daughter—she needed to find a place in her life for her ex-husband.

The Divorce Talk

A divorce tests the strength and resilience of the mother-daughter relationship more than any other hot-button issue—and the repercussions of this wrenching event last a lifetime. The best way you can ensure that your relationship with your daughter stays strong and healthy is to stay face-to-face with her. And remember:

- *Do* encourage your daughter to maintain her relationship with her father. It doesn't do anyone any good—and in fact it could do a great deal of harm—if her relationship with her dad is severely strained.

- *Do* try to stay on cordial terms with your ex. You may no longer be married, but you will be parenting this child together forever.

- *Don't* let your anger, resentment, hatred, or love of your ex cloud your relationship with your daughter. It's not easy, I know, but try your hardest. When you feel yourself wanting to say something unkind about your ex, *don't* say it. Your relationship with your daughter depends upon it.

There would be wonderful events in the future, events that the three of them would no doubt need to come together on. Nonetheless, helping a mom to understand and own how her unhealthy communication choices have affected the relationship she has with her daughter can be difficult, especially because most of the time she has made these unwise choices in hopes of creating a stronger relationship with her daughter.

One of my patients going through a divorce told me something that I will never forget. She was explaining to me how she knew it was time to leave her husband. At that point, although things weren't great between them, they weren't quite ready to take the next step. They prided themselves on the fact that their four-year-old daughter, Julia, never saw them fight or say unkind comments to each other, and they felt that as long as they were able to do this—to keep up the façade of the perfectly happy couple—they had time to figure things out. One night, as mom was tucking her into bed, Julia asked, "Why don't you love Daddy?" She was stunned by the question.

"Why would you ask me that?" Mom asked.

"Because you never tell him the way you tell me," she replied. "You never say 'I love you' to Daddy."

Julia was right. And it was extremely significant.

One of the most difficult challenges a mom faces within the dynamic of divorce is maintaining honest, open, and healthy communication with her daughter. Raw emotions for both of them complicate this challenge even more. The Chair Strategy can provide safety and a framework in which effective communication can take place and allow them to strengthen the mother-daughter bond during this difficult transition.

Epilogue

WE BEGAN THIS JOURNEY together with a leap of faith. I asked you to commit to a process that you knew little about. You did that. I asked you for honesty in your participation. You did that as well. And I asked for your trust that this process would bring you a positive result. You trusted me. My hope is that, in return, you feel as if you are truly at the beginning of a healthier relationship with not only your daughter but with yourself, based on love, understanding, and respect. This is what you both want, and as you continue to move toward the side-by-side position, this is what you both will have.

Make no mistake, the relationship you have with your daughter is and always will be a work in progress. Every day is a new challenge. Yesterday's problems and solutions will be replaced with new and unforeseen challenges. My hope is that the perspective you now have as a mom will continue to guide you in a healthy and loving direction with your daughter. The up-front work you have done and the tools you now have will support this direction, and will provide you with the strength, balance, and clarity you need to continue forever. I also hope that the close-up peek into the lives of other mother and daughters, at the very least, has reinforced that you are not alone.

Though this book has focused on you as a mom, let's remember now that you are also a daughter. You have experienced both sides of the equation this book describes. As a mother, you have been the one to reach out and embrace the ideas in this book and incorporate the Chair Strategy into your life so that you and your daughter could connect in a more loving way. And now that you are equipped with strength, balance, and clarity as a mother, I ask you to consider this in your role as daughter as well. Your mother may very well be reading this book along with you. I hope so. If not, here is an opportunity for you to resume your role as designated driver—only this time to reach out to your mom. It's worth considering.

Think of the lifelong journey with your daughter as if you were weathering a storm. While you forge on through rain and wind, you both yearn to be protected from the elements. Though each of you imagines a place of calm—lounging fireside, wrapped in a cozy blanket—it is you, mom, who knows the way there. When the stinging storms of life rain forcefully down, it is you who can soothe the thunder and provide the shelter your daughter needs. And there is nothing in the world that compares with the relief and comfort as you open the door after a rough stretch, both of your senses springing to life and the familiar fire and blanket within reach once again. You have arrived back home. You, mom, are that home.

The power you have is awesome. And it is endless. No matter where you are right now—regardless of your circumstances—you are among the most powerful forces on the planet. As an individual, you have the power to make anything happen within the unique relationship with your daughter. Together, with your daughter, there is nothing that the two of you cannot accomplish. Remember this as the two of you move forward one day at a time. The power was yours from the start. And I'm certain that you are now able to access that power in more effective and loving ways.

Your daughter awaits.

Acknowledgments

Honing my clinical skills over the past twenty years has resulted in the strategies and examples written about in the following pages. Yet in developing this book I am particularly indebted to the individuals and families who opened their lives to me and made themselves vulnerable as together we worked toward the goal of emotional well-being.

I also extend thanks to The Agency Group for giving *Side by Side* structure; Mindy Werner for giving it life and making it work; and a special thanks to my fantastic editor, Cynthia DiTiberio, at HarperOne. Most importantly, I would like to thank my family for their tireless support, wisdom, and guidance, for without them all of my efforts would be meaningless.